W9-DJN-566

THREE CHURCHES AND A MODEL T

Philip Jerome Cleveland

THREE CHURCHES AND A MODEL T

FLEMING H. REVELL COMPANY

Westwood, New Jersey
London E.C.4—29 Ludgate Hill
Glasgow C.2—229 Bothwell Street

Library of Congress Catalog Card Number: 60-5504

Printed in the United States of America

1.1

Part of the material in the chapter "Change of Cars" is reprinted by permission of *Christianity Today.*

The poem "Cricket" in the chapter "Song and Story" is reprinted by permission of *The Saturday Evening Post.*

The chapter "The Hour That Changed My World" is reprinted by permission of *Yankee Magazine* and was previously entitled "My Hour with Billy Phelps."

The chapters "Last Call to a Family" and "A Day at the Polls" are reprinted by permission of *The New Haven Register.*

The poem "By Night" is reprinted by permission of *Good Housekeeping Magazine.*

The chapter "Grove of Pines" is reprinted by permission of *The New England Homestead.*

The chapter "Chimes and Christmas Capers" is reprinted by permission from *Journal of Lifetime Living*, December, 1951 and was previously entitled "What It's Like to Play Santa Claus."

The poem "Prayer of a Pastor" is reprinted by permission of *This Week Magazine* and was previously entitled "Prayer."

To my beloved uncle
RUPERT DYER CHUTE
who taught me
melodies, magnitudes, ministries

Foreword

It is said that an honest confession is good for the soul. No doubt it is. As I place the finishing touches to this volume it is, confessedly, with a feeling of satisfaction.

Someone ought to relate, if he can, something of the multiple performances of a rural pastor in this troubled, bewildered, all but incredible world. I trust I have not done it badly.

Good metropolitans often envy the quiet, unruffled lives of their country cousins; city pastors, rectors and curates often sigh for the mild and mellow music which they fancy plays always in the rural fields.

Said Fulton Oursler to me one day as I sat talking with him in the cluttered study at the Hotel Navarro, overlooking Central Park: "The momentous, critical affairs of life have a strange way of making their entrance in the country. Philip, keep your ears on the ground, your eyes on the land. The city is often the last place to receive the divine word; the country is generally the spot where God makes His debut. It is interesting that the Nativity, the Baptism, the Sermon on the Mount have country backgrounds.

"Know your parish. One day you may have something to tell the busy, tired city dwellers. Take the country's pulse like a skillful doctor; keep your fingers on the life-throbs there, on the many stirring heartbeats. Be a good physician interested in the cure of souls. Write me what the pulse registers."

I did write him a few generalizations and, now and then, a

diagnosis. He has left the city and the country; but in loving memory I am sending on now a more or less complete report of my findings, hoping that I have not wholly failed to meet the challenge of a wise editor, a top-flight writer, a wonderful man.

PHILIP JEROME CLEVELAND

The Dille Larger Parish
Le Raysville, Pennsylvania

Contents

THREE CHURCHES AND A MODEL T

A Church That Stopped Talking

"Is the minister in?" a short, stocky man said to my wife on the sun-shot back steps to the manse one propitious Monday morning.

When I opened the door he smiled, a blue cap in hand, work overalls afire in the molten sun-glow. His whole attitude was one of forceful business. He recognized me. He had attended worship service only the day before.

"Say, preacher, do you really want that bell hung?" he challenged. "You said yesterday that the church had no voice. Perhaps I could get that old church talking again."

"Your name?" I suggested.

"Call me Hans—Pennsylvania Dutch vintage. I'm a truck driver. We have a two weeks' vacation on hand. Truck strike, out of Boston. I drive out of Boston every week. But I live in town. Right now the strike has thrown me out of a job."

The day before I had informed the Canterbury folks that we should rebuild the belfry smashed by the 1938 hurricane. Here it was, 1946, and the seven-hundred-pound bell still sat silent inside the large, green church doors. A building committee appointed in 1942 had not done a thing; it had apparently been stillborn. Reaction was exactly zero.

"You think you could build a church belfry?"

"Worked years for a construction company; served as head rigger for Bethlehem Steel. I might get that bell ringing for you. I'd have to get authority, I know."

"Well, you've got it!"

"You are giving me the green light?"

"I sure am. Come on, let's get going."

The 175th anniversary of Westminster Church was coming up in a few weeks. Why not ring out the old, ring in the new?

"Come on."

We visited the rambling, grey farmhouse of the senior deacon, Frederick A. Hicks.

"Come along," I enthused to Fred. "We're hanging the bell."

"Gracious, goodness, we are?" he stammered, sixty-five years of age and a bachelor. "How come?"

"We got an offer." Introducing Hans, I told the story. In fifteen minutes the three of us were at a sawmill deep in the tangled woodlands of Plainfield.

Said Hans to the owner of the mill: "I got to have three one-thousand-pound oak timbers."

"Ain't got 'em," was the brisk retort.

"You can get them," challenged Hans.

"Got to cut down fresh trees. Got to send my men into the woods."

"Cut them! Send them," boomed the enthusiastic truckman.

The next day, at dusk, three one-thousand-pound oak timbers and an assorted pile of lumber were stacked beneath the maple trees of the churchyard and the following morning Hans led his gang into the hurricane-smashed building. One youth was Russian, another a Norwegian, another a Frenchman, another Finnish, and still another a German.

Who were they? Where did they hail from? Who was paying their salaries?

The curious, ill-assorted strangers, a motley crew, smoking, grinning, joking, using rough language, entered the church, squirmed up in under the roof and began a most astonishing invasion of the upper air.

A church window was removed and through that second-floor opening thousand-pound timbers, two-by-fours, long, short, green, seasoned timber poured into the sanctuary.

These men twisted legs around planks, hung from beam-ends, scaled minimums of scaffolding, worked, laughed, joked and pounded nails, drove in rivets, lined up chalk-marks and slowly lifted a belfry toward the blue skies.

Hans was here, there, everywhere, directing, ordering, correcting, readjusting, superintending.

Two evenings after the work began, sitting in his kitchen as his good wife served sandwiches and coffee, I asked him about the blueprints.

"Blueprints?" he bellowed, leaning back in a chair, "I don't go for blueprints and architects. You know, preacher, what I got for plans?"

From a dirty shirt pocket he slowly drew forth a small scrap of paper with a dozen pencil marks across it.

"That's all the blueprint I have—up to now. More will come later after I dream over the problems. More always comes."

I still hear Hans calling to his buddies, "Hand me my persuasion," as the heavy hammer was shoved him for a stern blow. He would join one huge timber to another and triumph: "Yes, sir, she's my baby!" When a particular assignment had been completed he would exult, "Just like New York!"

"Time to refuel," he would say at 11:50. And how he did refuel! He would sweat all morning and then send to the village store for two quart bottles of soda pop for dinner—huff, puff, he would sweat and grunt satisfaction as he sat drinking the pop on the wide church steps.

The carriage, the rocker of the bell, had been smashed by the hurricane. How to get the old Pilgrim bell to rocking and rolling? Hans wrestled with this problem for a week. One morning he cried to two members of his crew: "Let's go to Norwich to the junkyards. I got me an idea."

Two hours later he returned to the churchyard with an iron skeleton of something tied to the front of his car, a diamond-shaped thing, a tubular, dry-bone sort of thing.

"What on earth?" I gasped.

"Preacher, there's the vocal cords to your church!" he triumphed. "Yes, sir, she's my baby!"

He struggled with another man to lift the queer auto-part, the funny skeleton-thing, upstairs, and soon the seven-hundred-pound bell was making strident, incredible music high atop Westminster hill.

"Well, what is that thing anyway?" I demanded. "It's some part of an auto."

"Just call it a yo-yo!" he laughed, slapping a pal on the back. "It's the most practical and original bell-rocker in the world!"

Shall I ever forget the day that two solemn members of the inactive building committee slowly climbed ladders to gaze on the motley crew in full operation high in the incredibly evolving belfry and to listen to the infernal racket?

"Reverend, how is it that these men are here?"

"I invited them."

"On what authority?"

I quoted a famous passage from David Lloyd George, the embattled British premier: "The finest eloquence is that which gets things done; the worst is that which delays them."

One remarkable day, some weeks later, Fulton Oursler arrived at the manse and accompanied me to Westminster Church. He had driven with his wife, Grace Perkins Oursler, from New York City. I had written to him about our all but incredible doings in northeastern Connecticut. Interested, he had come on. After lunch he sat with me and listened to the rain on the church roof. He took a chair in the balcony and stared through a hole at an uprising belfry as I narrated the amazing story.

"Philip," he suggested, "where do you suppose Hans dug up that ill-assorted crew? I believe we have the real kernel of a story right there. The *Digest* might publish it—if we can ascertain the plain facts of the case. Hans didn't just walk out doors and bump into those fellows. How, where and when did the Dutchman assemble that crew which worked for nothing?"

Oursler had a wonderful sniff for a story, and he was adamant about tracing down a clue. He never surrendered a writer's hunch until every possible means had been exhausted. Until he learned the basic facts he would not even try to get the story of "The Broken Bell" into the columns of *Reader's Digest*.

"Hans, where did you round up that gang?" I begged.

For years the saints had prayed and hoped and nothing had happened. Then suddenly, out of the blue, a stranger had climbed a back porch and a man unchurched had gone forth, a two weeks' strike on his hands, to marshal the unlikely crew. Indeed, as Deacon Hicks had asked, how come?

"Ask my wife about it," Hans replied. He would say nothing more. His wife would grin sheepishly and tell me to inquire of the Russian. The Russian would emit a self-conscious grin and refer me to the Norwegian, who sent me off to find the Frenchman. The Frenchman thought the German had the proper version.

For weeks I rode this fast and futile merry-go-round. One day I complained to Hans that he didn't want the church to succeed. He was killing the success story.

"Me?" he bellowed. "Who got that church talking again? Who figured out that yo-yo? Why, you can pull on that bell rope today and there's no vibration anywhere. When they used to pull on the rope, the church shook enough to rattle a guy's false teeth!"

"I know, Hans, *but where did you get the help?*"

"Listen, preacher; that belfry is so sturdy that the next hurricane will take the church and leave the belfry!"

"I've got to know where you found those men," I persisted.

"Preacher, you wouldn't want to know."

"I must know."

After tremendous pressure Hans made a statement.

"Well, preacher, I couldn't get help. Tried a whole day. So I went to the tavern and handed those guys a bit of a sermon myself. I said, 'Come on! Let's give the preacher a break! Let's do one decent thing before we're all dead! A poor preacher's got a nice old bell that's a deaf-mute. Let's perform an operation and put a tongue in it! Whaddya say, fellows?' " He paused a moment and concluded: "And, by gosh, they did!" Hans looked searchingly into my ministerial eyes.

In a few moments he ventured an anticlimax.

"Don't it sound crazy? Do you wonder nobody wanted to talk? And now—are you satisfied? Or shall I tell you some more?"

"Enough!" I cried. "Enough's enough!"

Frightened, I carried that grim, bewildering confession to Fulton Oursler.

"I knew it, I knew it! I just knew there was a great story behind that construction crew."

"You consider that a great story?" I stuttered.

"I most certainly do," he said.

We did have the success story and Fulton grinned later as I quoted a favorite quatrain to him:

It's a good thing to remember
   And a better thing to do;
To work with the construction gang
   And not the wrecking crew.

Change of Cars

Center Church, Congregational, in New Britain, Connecticut, was having a big day; in its pulpit was the widely-known radio preacher, S. Parkes Cadman of Brooklyn. The pews were packed; it was a meeting of men, with whom Dr. Cadman was always at his best. He was introduced by the pastor of Center Church, Dr. Theodore Ainsworth Greene, a fine preacher never at a loss for words, and no mean orator.

His introductory remarks began in good style—Dr. Greene was quietly effective in his "slow start." But soon he was rising to the occasion with his unfailing and irresistible eloquence. He said that he had recently been backstage in a huge radio station, where he had gazed long and reverently on bewildering electrical instrument boards, switches, batteries, tubes, generators and flashing lights. He had even seen sparks, somewhere in the labyrinth, flashing here and there as lively evidence of these "powers of the air," and he made the best use possible of these sparks in a pun concerning "S. Parkes . . . ." He wove a neat web of words.

As he accelerated in eloquence, no doubt there came to his mind one of those phrases that seem so apt while one is speaking and only in retrospect reveal a trap. The phrase came straight from the Epistle to the Ephesians, where St. Paul pictures "the prince of the power of the air, the spirit that now worketh in the children of disobedience" (2:2). Grasping the phrase and momentarily forgetting the original connection, Dr. Greene enthused:

"Think of the radio ministry of Dr. Cadman, and his amazing influence spread over the air waves of the nation as he talks every Sunday afternoon! Millions listen, spellbound! I have introduced many prominent speakers to this congregation, but I am happy on this rare occasion to introduce the king of the electrons, the ruler of the airways—in fact, the prince of the power of the air, Dr. S. Parkes Cadman!"

Dr. Cadman pulled himself to his feet from a cushioned, high-backed chair; he seemed almost to stagger to the sacred desk. It was a strange tense moment; it found the radio minister wordless—a real phenomenon. When he recovered his voice, he said slowly, "Gentlemen, I have been introduced to many audiences and with many compliments, but this is the first time I have ever been released upon a waiting audience as His Majesty, the Devil!"

Deeply impressed and stirred by his address, I drove home over the Connecticut hills, in a noticeably deepening fog. From Willimantic on, it was so thick that I moved like a snail. It was late when I pulled into my driveway. I was tired. Why bother to put the car in the garage on such a night? Nobody could see the house, let alone the car. I left it there—and so to bed.

In the morning I went out to take an umbrella and some books from the car. I stared east, west, north, south. Where on earth had I mislaid my automobile? It is rather a bulky object to mislay. Yes, there was the maple tree, the open garage. But where, oh where, had my little car gone? The large, cordwood pile, stacked for saw-rigging, did not shelter a fender.

Only last week Bruce, our freckle-faced baby boy, had stood on an empty orange crate and had preached to the cordwood pile. Mother, seeing him silhouetted in a burst of sunlight, had rushed outdoors.

"Bruce, what is going on?"

"I'm preaching just like Daddy."

"What do you mean?"

"Isn't this a lumberyard now, mother?"

"Well, yes."

"Didn't Daddy say that preaching to empty pews is the same as preaching to a lumberyard?"

Well, no one had molested four cords of oak, cherry, birch, hickory. But where was the car hiding? Had the brakes failed and had it plunged down the nearby slope? No. It was not a wreck against the stone wall.

I called the state police, reporting a Connecticut cleric as the latest victim of the ever-present car thieves. The prince of the power of the air had been about, it seemed, not only in a city congregation, but over the dark, rural hills as well.

The mystery was never quite solved. Many days later my auto was found, abandoned, stripped, on a grimy New York City wharf. A neighbor said he barely noticed two thin, scrawny hitchhikers near my driveway as his headlamps tried to pierce the dense fog very late that fateful night.

The weekly paper carried the story of a rural pastor's

dilemma—no means of transit and a circuit of growing churches on his hands. The following morning my phone rang three times. A printer, a jeweler, a tire-shop boss offered cars to the immobilized pastor.

Wilhelm Heinzman—Willie—placed the first call, and I leaped to accept his offer. I had met him in jail. Now and then a long-suffering Willie, of German background, attempted to discipline a cantankerous wife and two stout sons, for which the judge always gave him thirty days in which to re-think his household policies.

"I got a Model T, preacher. I don't need it. I drive to work with Sam. I'll run it right over. Use it till you get your own jalopy back."

Willie displayed his jalopy with manifest pride and joy. It had once been black. What was its precise color now? Years ago as a young theological student, I liked one pair of black trousers. I enjoyed pressing them until they turned a kind of sour-apple green. Was this the color of the faded old Model T?

Well, we established quite an acquaintance, traveling the helter-skelter Connecticut hills in all kinds of weather, for better and for worse, for richer and poorer.

One church stood, white and stately, just around the corner, the structure where Priest Whitney once ministered so bravely to his people. The small Westford Hill Congregational Church straddled a green eminence thirty miles to the northwest; Millington Green Church, where David Brainerd, world-famous missionary once preached, loomed on another hill thirty miles to the southwest. Three churches and a model T! A sad sour-apple-green car and a blessed earthly trinity of aging churches crying for attention! What a time we all had for a while together!

It seemed that every curious canine along highways and byways barked at a car and a cleric. The car did seem, at times, especially at dusk, to suggest the ghost of a vehicle. Boys pelted its faded paint with pebbles; girls grinned and pointed at it; old folks halted their progress beside rural roads to stand and stare. We must have been obvious, a large man in preacher-black with a gaily-bonneted wife in the front seat; four sprightly, howling youngsters tucked in back.

One night I returned to the manse from a particularly trying, exhausting day. We came in on a wheel and a prayer—a steaming, wobbling car and its grim occupant. The wheezing vehicle tottered up the stony driveway and limped to a staggering stop.

Wendell—brown, tousled Wendell, seven years old—was playing in the sunset-yard. He observed everything.

"Daddy," he ventured, "Daddy, didn't you say you *loved* your church work?"

"Yes, I have said that. But why?"

"Then is this what the song means when it tells about the *bumpety road to love?*"

I cannot imagine from this remote date what I said in answer to my son's wistful question.

And yet I was not wholly miserable the day I left the grey-green phantasy in a cluttered rural yard. I thanked Willie for his many tender mercies though every bone in my body ached. To this day, I am grateful to Willie for standing as a great help in time of need, and I am deeply respectful to Mr. Ford, who most certainly sparked an industrial revolution in his mass production of the lowly Model T, one of which came to Willie, and from Willie to me. I trust Willie will understand when I say that, grateful and respectful as I was, I was not too unhappy when at long last I left the apple-green rattler in his yard and turned from it for the last time, leaving a blessing upon it: "May you rest in peace!"

The Frightful Sabbath

Dog days, one humid August Sunday, almost took toll of my little boy's life. Even now, as I sit staring at a country weekly's screaming headline, I do some serious thinking.

> VICIOUS DOG ALMOST FATALLY WOUNDS PREACHER'S SMALL SON FOLLOWING CHURCH SERVICE. FOURTH CHILD ATTACKED IN TWO DAYS. ANOTHER CHILD BITTEN A YEAR AGO.

The whole day's experience was dramatic, crucial—the children singing in the manse before Sunday school, the sun shining at half-mast, shall we say, apparently low and dim through the thick humidity. My sermon subject seemed to brand me a false prophet (that, too, got worked into the weekly newspaper): "The Day Will Hold Some Lovely Thing." That was the sermonic theme; the text was found in the book of Psalms: "This is the day which the Lord hath made; we will rejoice and be glad in it."

About half of the largest audience the church had welcomed in August for many years had vanished from lush green lawns and thin maple shadows. The remainder were enjoying a social moment when a child's scream of terror startled the loiterers.

I knew that voice!

My seven-year-old son, the baby boy Bruce, was in trouble. From the front steps of the Westminister Church I rushed past cars toward the rear cemetery. A church deacon, Verne, had seized a large dog in his bare hands and was flinging, kicking him against the graveyard fence.

Bruce bent over on the green grass.

"He is only scared!" I exclaimed, hoping for the best.

"Dear God!" screamed Elsie, the Willimantic beauty. "His mouth is full of blood!"

Bruce was trying to keep the crimson flow from a brand-new white shirt and tie. He was so proud of them! His older brother and sister raced to the scene. His mother reached the boy and froze, almost paralyzed with fear. The dog had bitten twice—into the left cheek and under the jaw, close to the jugular vein.

"Get to a phone, call Willimantic Hospital! Tell them to have everything ready! It will take fifteen minutes to arrive!" Elsie issued orders to her brother-in-law. To her husband she yelled: "Get in the car!" She pushed me into the front seat and helped Bruce into the back.

Noting my wife's panic, I said: "He'll be all right. Where's your faith?"

"I've got it, *but hurry, honey!*"

Never shall I forget those words.

Elsie used up two handkerchiefs, holding layers of the cheek together, forcing the divided flesh of his throat to come together, her fingers making human pincers. Bruce spoke only once in transit.

"Daddy, is it very much farther?"

Elsie's brother-in-law had called the hospital which, in turn, had called a nearby physician. He was in the operating room when we arrived and went to work immediately.

Handing Bruce a shiny nickel I promised: "You will have more if you are brave." I challenged: "And I'll take you to the wayside stand for a hot-dog supper when you get home."

The doctor put four stitches in the cheek and three in the throat. "A third attack would have finished him," mused the sober physician.

Sewing the throat, the needle broke. Bruce winced, swallowed, his face went white, but there was no outcry. The doctor swung around to me.

"Few adults have the stamina of that boy!" he judged. "He ought to be one of Doug MacArthur's men." He turned back to Bruce. "You're a real leatherneck!"

Nothing was administered to the child to freeze or etherize the wound. There just wasn't time.

The moment the doctor left, the wistful, bright-eyed boy said to me: "The more I pray, the quicker I'll get well."

Elsie had no children. She now came close to me, tears swimming in sea-blue eyes, touched a hand and confessed: "Do you realize, Reverend, that you have a *saint* in your house? Oh, if, if *I* only had a kid like that!" She could not find another word to say. In her handsome Sunday-go-to-meeting duds she sailed like a proud, glorious ship out of the grim harbor of a hospital room.

As her husband hurried me back to Canterbury to the tense

family waiting at the manse, I bemoaned the unfortunate turn of events. I had pledged that the day would hold some lovely thing and behold, terror and tragedy. Elsie turned her blue-white prisms upon me with an ironic toss of head.

"You think, Reverend, that the day didn't hold some lovely thing? Didn't you discover the kind of a kid you've got? The doctor was thrilled. I know he was. Talk about courage, faith, fortitude, strength. Why, everything you talked about this morning, that kid lived, proved, an hour later! Oh, if I ever had a kid like that!" And once more the elegant, glamorous lady of thirty-five found herself lost for words.

Bruce was treated for rabies. The dog did not have the dread disease.

Later, Elsie's husband, Verne, hunted down the killer, a mixture of shepherd and collie, which snarled and bared its teeth, but was overcome by the good deacon, a powerful construction man. Verne's aged father accompanied him in quest of the merciless attacker. Later he had confessed to being a bit shaky as Verne drove the canine into a back seat and carried him to a veterinarian.

"Think of it!" he confessed, trembling. "That terrible creature in the back seat and my neck right in front!"

The state beheaded the would-be killer, but there was no sign of rabies or other ailment. He was just a vicious animal that disliked children. The dog warden had ordered his owner, who lived three miles away, to keep the dog tied. He had broken his chain over the week end and like a ghoul had dashed from the graveyard to claim my son.

Except for the heroic efforts of a childless couple I would have lost my child. Later, God blessed Verne and Elsie with a most handsome and engaging son.

Indeed, the day did hold its lovely thing. But it takes sometimes a childless, empty-armed woman to show a most fortunate pastor the vast treasures that flit about a sunny church lawn and fill a humble rural manse!

I am not reluctant to confess that, one August Sabbath morning in rural Connecticut, I was forced to endure my greatest test of faith!

The Magic of a Word

Cried an ancient, lonely man in time of sorrow and tragedy: "How forcible are right words!"

I think of Job's stirring declaration when I think of a long, dusty road in Connecticut, and a man of weariness and sadness, far from his native haunts, a man unloved, unwept and unsung by acres of American farmers.

You see, he was a Russian, an immigrant farmer from an unpopular sector of the world. He did not care for slaughter on his verdant hills and forbade any deer hunting, whether in season or not. His three fierce dogs refused to permit any car, never mind the make or style, to pass unchallenged past his premises.

A Dutchman in a jeep came to a noisy stop in a spiraling cloud of dust as I started up a hilly road. I had motioned to him.

"Who lives along the road?" I inquired.

He mentioned a half-dozen names and then advised: "Don't bother with the first place. They're Russians, plenty ornery. Nobody ever stops there. The man's the meanest cuss I ever met. Won't let us cross the land, or fish, or shoot a buck. Nobody has dealings with him. He's likely to sick the dogs on you."

The three ferocious canines did most certainly challenge transit, five minutes later. It was clear that the creatures, like the Russian, had no respect for the church. The howling furies headed for the car, jumped, bared fangs, tried to bite the rubber tires to pieces and only a burst of speed and deluging them in dust removed me from mishap.

Three times I passed by the large, grey-white farmhouse and the huge, red barn in a hurry, barely noticing the cows, the pastures, the fields of silage-corn.

Said the neighbors: "You'd never get them to church. They're heathen! They don't mingle with anyone; they won't talk to anybody. They'd only insult you for your trouble. Better ride right by, Reverend."

On the fourth trip, close to sundown, passing the forbidden precincts, one dog snapping at a front wheel, I suddenly spied a large, stocky shadow emerging from a barn door, a cane in one hand, the other hand holding a thick sandwich to a bewhiskered face. His eye happened to meet mine as my car came alongside the barn.

Life is unpredictable. The man seemed lonely, weary, tragic as he loomed in that barn door. The face was just that of an ordinary, hard-pressed farmer; the form of homespun was certainly of a harmless variety. I knew one word of Russian, learned in Connecticut. I called it through an open car window.

"*Tovarich.*"

It is a Russian word meaning comrade, friend.

That large, sturdy form straightened, the eyes stared, the sandwich was lowered; it was waved toward me in a simple, rural gesture. He beckoned me to stop the car.

"How you know that word?" he questioned, a queer, puzzled look on his face.

"A Russian cossack friend and a Russian countess, living only a few miles away, taught me Russian."

"You know my language?"

"One word."

Linguists may stare aghast at my stock-in-trade of language and wonder how a single word became the "Open Sesame" to the entire farm, the cattle, the pastures, the hay crops, the lush fields, even to a truce with the three furies. After the master scolded them properly, they permitted the church car to proceed unmolested and according to plan.

"You like to see barn, new milk house?" he asked.

"Delighted, sir."

Arthritis was troubling him and he confessed he doubted if he could carry on the heavy farm chores many more months.

"Wife is ill . . . in house. Her limbs worse than mine. We not young . . . any more."

In twenty minutes he said that he must go and call the cattle home. He had enjoyed talking with somebody. His married children lived at considerable distances and one did get lonely just to pass the time of day with a friend. "You call again, when I not so busy, and mebbe wife . . . she be able to see you."

I returned home, a sentence from a wonderful old Book singing in my consciousness: "I have called you friends."

A month later I spied him crossing the dusty road from the

farmhouse to barn. He thrust forth a strong hand when I approached.

"Preacher, I feel a little better. Hay is in barn, corn in silo."

He sat on the grassy, colorful autumn slope, the cane at his side.

"But knees not so young, preacher. Hips, ankles get old. So I sit down and rest . . . if you excuse."

In a few moments a small but stout, attractive woman limped across the road, three dogs escorting her. She labored in walking and stood by the roadside.

"My man, he told me you called and saw barn. I like to meet . . . priest."

While we talked farm topics, hay, milk gallonage, markets, supply and demand, the neighbors' cars roared past. Not a friendly, kindly eye turned like a lower light burning to a man of seventy and an aged wife of seventy-one. Two world-weary and sick, burdened people were aware of their isolation. I could not but notice this.

I wonder if I recalled an ancient Palestinian prescription for just such an hour as this? "Come unto me, all ye that labour and are heavy laden, and I will give you rest." I did think of many things, my Master's ethic and two dear, strange people called "contraband" in their green, beautiful hills where once Pilgrims and Indians met in genial fellowship.

Did the white-haired lady with the pale, wrinkled face divine my thoughts? I have wondered ever since. In that solemn, sad hour she made a statement that I shall carry with me to the grave.

"Priest, we are religious people, Greek Orthodox. I have Bible, prayer book, icons. I have shrine in bedroom corner. I pray to God. I believe in Jesus Christ our Lord."

"You never attend church?" I suggested, wistfully.

"You like to know why . . . priest?"

"I would like to know."

"Well, these people, neighbors, you see how they hurry by? They hate us. They hate my man because he not want bloodshed on his hills, because he will not use bad language, because he keep dogs so people not steal heifer, chicken.

"God tell us to love, did He not?" How she searched my eyes and face!

"Yes, that is in the gospel."

"If I go to their church, I make them hate. They see me, my man, they glare at us, their hearts be hard toward us. They hate. How can they, if they hate, worship the God who only comes to us if we love?

"So I stay home . . . alone . . . and pray . . . that my neighbors may please God when they worship. I like church, organ, choir, sermon. But if I only make people hate, I only hurt church. So I stay home and pray . . . that the church, some time, find that love come to it."

Yes, this was an actual statement from a white Russian lady of the far Ukraine. It was a tremendous sermon proclaimed by a sick, aging woman in most humble cloth along life's long and dusty way; that road might well have been the road to Emmaus, Bethany, Bethabara.

Her husband, trying to find bodily peace on the grassy slope, groaned and rubbed his knees. I knelt by the long, hard way and prayed, my hands on a poor farmer's arthritic knees, great, rubber boots enclosing the legs.

"O great God, help this man, Thy servant, to do his honest work in this world, to call his cattle home, to keep his Christian acres. O blessed Traveler from far Nazareth, strengthen our brother and enable him to arise and walk as Thou didst challenge other hard-pressed people in times gone by."

One car whirred by in a blinding cloud of dust and it was plain to see that the curious riders had no inkling of wayside devotions and an honest home missions attempt.

When the little prayer was finished I gave hand to a lame man, not beside the beautiful gate of a celebrated temple, but to one surrounded by the staggering beauty of October hills.

"Priest, next time you call . . . we receive you in house," enthused the lady of the Ukraine. "We be in to you."

And I am also hoping and praying, alongside of two old, loving hearts, that the Eternal Love will soon make it possible for two lonely people to find their highest worship experience in the Christian Church. They find it so hard to sing the Lord's songs alone and in a lonely land.

Should they enter our sanctuary some clear, bright Sabbath morning, I would call for the singing of a tender and very beautiful hymn, appropriate for the occasion: "O Love that will not let me go."

He Came to Me a Suicide

"Are you going to be in for an hour or two? It's mighty important. I got to see you."

The voice was that of Jud Hawkins, his grandfather Chief Fast Runner and Swimmer of the Mohegan village in Montville. I had preached in the little, white-towered Indian church. For some twenty years I had known Jud and this was his first move toward the church or manse.

The call came at 8:30 and about a half-hour later Jud stepped into the living room. He was haggard, nervous, his thick, black hair a scraggly mess, his deep-set, black eyes unsteady, his leatherlike cheeks deeply lined with anxiety.

It seemed he could not wait to unburden himself.

"Parson, I'm in a terrible jam. I've been arrested. The police have moved in. They've learned that I'm not married to Nan and that Sonny isn't mine on the books. I'm all ready for a trip to the big house. My dad put up the bail pending court, but I can't raise a red cent to hire a lawyer. Without a lawyer the judge will throw the book at me. I'm in a terrible mess!"

Jud was of average size, at present unusually stout, powerfully built, not corpulent. His neck was thick, heavy like a Guernsey bull's. His skin was dark, the teeth large, uneven, the lips thick, the mouth large. When he talked the scarred, discolored teeth became unpleasantly obvious. The thick lips rolled apart as though in labor; one almost thought of a woman in the clutch of childbirth now as he struggled to get out his confession.

"Nan has a husband and three kids in New York state. He was a brute; she left him. I picked her up five years ago; we decided to try life together."

Jud's first wife had been slain by a hit and run driver, some twenty years earlier, on a great Connecticut highway, while going to work one morning. It was a fearful story. By a curious twist of fate I had covered that tragedy for the press with stories and photos.

Jud had been a heavy drinker but by sheer will power had overcome his enemy. He had often shoved the police around when they annoyed him; as a politician he had wielded power in fairly high places. Now he loomed before me on a parlor chair like a huge animal at bay, cornered, cowering, sensing imminent judgment.

"The kid is mine, parson. We all know it. He's the one thing I got to give the world worth talking about. I got just one decent thing to hand over from this dirty mess. I got to do right by that kid!"

This theme, on which he placed real, persistent emphasis, stirred my soul. Cannot a man envision a tremendous stellar space with an eye fixed to a single lens? Suddenly heroism glimmered out of a vast expanse of moral ruin and basic, elemental light trembled from the darkness.

"Parson, all I got in the world is . . . that kid. But I got to have money; I got to have a lawyer."

"Your parents own their home, don't they?"

"Dad is old, sick; he's put up my bail. He can't do more."

"Your sister works."

"The mill is on part time."

"Your brother has a good position."

"And many children."

"Your other sister?"

"She's dead broke."

"You've got lots of friends."

"I thought I did have. I've made the rounds, for nothing." He repeated the grim judgment. "For nothing."

"You know, Jud, I get only forty dollars a week here and have to pay all my utilities. I have four children and am putting one boy through seminary."

"Listen, parson. I've been everywhere, tried everything. There was only one thing left—the church. For the first time in my life I thought I'd try the church."

I am going to say here something I didn't say to Jud. I don't think people play fair and square with the church. For instance, a Boy Scout commissioner once called on the church to pour forth healing prayers for a child when the most experienced medical knowledge despaired of his life.

A family appealed to me—it was an initial move toward any sanctuary—to save many children from delinquency when the state was cleaning every one out of a morally bankrupt home.

An emotionally hysterical mother asked me to tell God to send her girl home when for three and one-half years her best friends had lost all contact with her. If I knew God, her girl must be home by New Year's eve; she gave me three months to prevail.

Now here was Jud coming to the manse for the miracle! When he challenged the church to prove itself he had, of course, probed deeply under my skin.

"I thought you might scrape up two hundred and fifty," he continued.

"It doesn't grow on trees."

Jud bent his tangled crop of hair to two grim, dusky hands and for a moment flood tides of pent-up emotion burst all barriers and poured in over the rim of the hidden seas. He rocked in the seething impact of climactic sorrow. His body shook as the shore in the claw of the tempest. When he regained a measure of poise he made a frightful statement. It seemed a shadow fell aslant his face, as though high above somewhere a thick cloud concealed all stellar spaces.

"I know what I can do," he confessed slowly, his face tense, his black eyes determined; there was a certain precision in his voice that seized upon me like steel clamps. "I have home a little bottle of poison. I have kept it on hand. That will take care of me. I'm a failure, a fool, and I knew this whole thing would backfire. How can I marry a woman not divorced? It's hard to get a divorce in New York state. There are some more things, not good, that will come out in court. I'm no doubt headed for the big house and I can't take it!"

His words were red-hot, burning things; the man became literally "terrific" in this dramatic moment. He edged his chair toward mine.

"What I have, parson, I'll leave the kid. I don't know if Nan is the one to bring him up . . . without me. I have to steady Nan sometimes. Pastor, what about that kid? He's going to have a jailbird for a father if I live!"

There are certain hours when a Bible verse can lean with awful weight upon the inner consciousness of a country parson.

"Comfort ye, comfort ye my people, saith the Lord. Speak ye comfortably to Jerusalem."

No word of mine reached the vulnerable spot.

Jud grinned a sad, desperate grin.

"I know you can't scrape up the two fifty, pastor. Sorry to trouble you with this rotten mess. Just thought I'd try the church." He shrugged huge, sagging shoulders. "There ain't no way out—except the one I told you about."

"You'd abandon ship in the storm?" I challenged. Jud had been a sailor for some years in an earlier time.

Silent, stern, desperate he glared at me.

"You will abandon that precious cargo—woman and child—in the dirty blow? Jud, is that your idea of seamanship?"

"Parson, hear me! I'm cornered, weak, afraid. I thought I'd never be weak and afraid. But I am!"

He jerked his heavy bulk from the parlor chair and moved on and into the kitchen. He was leaving the manse by way of the back door, a dark door facing an impenetrable wilderness road. I had not witnessed such misery, dejection in mortal man; I have not observed such anguish since. Heavily he moved across the kitchen floor like a man condemned, in chains. And he had . . . tried . . . church.

Possibly the words of a Nazareth Carpenter, pounding against the inner ear, had something to do with the finding of courage.

Let me make another observation.

Is it not strange, amazing, that in black moments of tremendous crisis, the words of a Jewish teacher on an Asiatic hill should prove to be the order of the day—not remembered advice of parents, the ethics of professors, the creeds of shrewd, living friends? In the kitchen, as a man limped across it to a door of night, words rose, rumbled in consciousness across the vast chasms of two thousand years.

"Give, and it shall be given unto you; good measure, pressed down, and shaken together, and running over, shall men give into your bosom."

It was brought to mind with the knowledge that I had saved a sum of two hundred and fifty dollars towards my son's seminary tuition. This amount was not yet due.

"Jud," I said, "I have the money. It is, in a sense, my son's money. It is indeed church money. I will loan it to you. I cannot, of course, ever press you for it. Personally, I think you might do better in this case without a lawyer. Go to court and give a simple, forthright statement of all the sad facts."

"Oh, parson, I got to have a lawyer. I wouldn't stand no chance at all without a lawyer!"

"If you insist—"

"Got to have a lawyer!" he interrupted. "It's my only chance!"

"Excuse me a moment, Jud."

Was it easy to give, in a moment, money saved through many months of painful denials, money equipping a son to assume care of my country's churches? No, it was not easy. The stewardship of silver is sometimes a great headache. Was I prepared to give beautiful measure? The Greek word in the text is beauty, not goodness.

All I know is that when Jud was handed the desired sum, the star-studded night made swift, brave intrusion of his eyes; the beauty of the heavens fell within two bleary, swollen eyes and a face dark, sombre, desperate, shone as in the full blaze of a summer moon.

Jud broke down and cried like a baby. At the door he

grasped my hand; it felt like steel and he blurted: "Shoulda tried church long time before."

His last words were: "You'll get every cent, with interest!"

The lawyer bungled the case; his learned, erudite evasions hurried his Indian client to state's prison. Had Jud made a simple, frank confession he would, no doubt, have spent but a short time in the county jail.

Jud began to read his Bible, to pray, to talk about God, mercy, faith, the divine goodness, to the inmates. He started a weekly prayer meeting within the formidable walls of the state prison. The jail ministry of the man with Mohegan blood in him was simply astonishing. He tried to help dope addicts, gangsters, bank robbers, killers. He insisted that I preach occasionally to the boys.

Shall I ever forget my first attempt to capture the minds of 150 men in state prison one clear Sabbath morning?

How to begin? Finally the right attack suggested itself. To men under heavy guard I announced: "You fellows haven't yet learned to put up a real fight."

I noted instantly that I had their attention.

"You pack revolvers, automatics, sawed-off shot guns; you take pot-shots at patrolmen and sheriffs, but you haven't yet fought a man-sized war."

"Whaddya mean?" growled one surly, podgy inmate in the rear.

"You shoot an unsuspecting cop, you beat your wives, whip your kids, beat up your pals, but you haven't drawn a dead-bead on the devil yet. You haven't yet got your real enemy in your sights.

"You haven't discovered, hunted down, destroyed your real foes—the things in your own lives that cripple, confine, devastate. Why don't you get wise and fight the real foes?

Aren't you big enough, smart enough, tough enough? Why, you're a bunch of kids with toy pistols aiming at paper targets!"

One colored man, a thin, straggly sort of a man, groaned, "O, God!" in a front seat, annoying his neighbors. We had quite a battle that Sabbath morning.

Jud is now saving hard cash to pay Nan's passage from a New York separation to a Connecticut marriage.

"Sonny will never have to walk the thorny path of his dad," swears the Indian, paroled, working, happy. On his face today is the light never seen on sea or land, as Wordsworth has written. His aged parents, his brother, sisters, the neighbors are all blinking eyes at it.

Has the beautiful measure returned unto my bosom?

What do *you* think?

Song and Story

There is no explanation for the sudden, contrasting transitions in life. Sun may halo a gorgeous summer field; in a few moments strange shadows may capture it so stealthily! And one has not divined the possibility of shadows, yet there they are!

One elegant September day a shiny, imposing limousine stopped at the small, white manse at the crossroads.

"No, the minister is not in," my wife revealed, answering the door.

"Where is he?"

"He's in the woodlot."

"Where is that?"

My wife gave careful directions.

Two hours earlier, equipped with axe, a small pad of paper and pencil, I had invaded the fragrant forest.

For years I cleared woodlots for farmers. They were making pastures: I received the gift of cut wood for my services. The exercise was healthful, the free fuel appreciated and in the beautiful solitudes I often found inspiration. I did this day.

Sitting on a log of fallen timber to rest after an hour with my axe, I became aware of the Mr. Johnny One-Note of the Connecticut thickets. A cricket was handing himself a time. His rapture filled the vast oratorio of nature. Suddenly the queer, strident little creature seemed to be in communication with me and pencil and pad came to hand. I recalled my brother's first three-quarter violin and his early days of intense practice.

Cricket, what a boy you are!
Crazy with joy,
Seizing on your very first
Tune like a boy.

Sawing, scraping all day long
Notes, harsh and thin,
Like a little boy with his
First violin.

Grinding out one tune until
Shepherds and sheep
And all the listening world fall
Exhausted asleep.

A sheep bell tinkled in a nearby pasture.

Wrapped in the light and inspiration of the experience, I was at first insensible to the intrusion of a police car. An auto horn shattered my bright revery. Shadows covered the hour. A girl of thirteen was destined to become a mother.

A policewoman sitting beside the patrolman handed me a sad confession to read. It was written crudely, badly; the thought-forms were worse. Four boys were named and all had vanished with the armed forces. What did I think? Did I know the girl? Did I know the boys?

What a darling, delightful girl she had been as she graduated from grade school, a vision in shining white, only one year earlier! Realizing that she had not attended church or Sunday school, I had urged her father at that time to give some thought to her developing girlhood, to permit her some religious training.

"I'm too busy, Reverend. The girl is needed in the strawberry patch, in the peach and apple orchard. She helps me trucking week ends. I need her now. Mebbe later I can spare her."

"But, Bill, she needs to know the Ten Commandments *now*, the Sermon on the Mount, the good way of life. She needs the right kind of companions today."

"I reckon I can take care of her, Reverend. I try to keep all my kids in hand. I'm not much for church, as you know. I really need her myself. The church will have to wait. Mebbe later."

"You're making a big mistake," I concluded as he turned away.

"I don't think so."

And now, many months later, in a haunt of timeless beauty, I read a girl's bitter, sickening confession.

Giving the officials what little information I could, offering what paltry aid I could, "cricket" stuck in my pocket, axe in hand, I hurried to the girl's house. The frantic, white-faced mother burst into lamentation.

"Why has God done this to us?" she wailed and argued. "Why should a scandal like this come to our house?"

"You never showed interest in the Lord's House," I said simply.

"We were too busy. Bill said he couldn't spare her and I never go against my man."

"She needed the church."

"That could be, pastor. But there was no telling my man that she did. I have heard her beg him to take her to church Sunday mornings. But he always took her to the garden, the orchard, on his trucking trips. She helped load boxes and sell things. She was always a good worker."

When Bill returned from work, I ran over to have a few words with him. What was he going to do about the girl?

"Let the law take its course," he replied. "It's all a no-good story. She should have known better. She has made her bed; let her lie in it. I'm sorry. She should have known better. The state has taken her. All of us got to live and learn."

In most cases of juvenile delinquency I have found the trouble some delinquent parent, usually a careless, unimaginative or selfish mother. In this instance it was the father who was responsible for the brutal shipwreck of a young and shining life. Bill was not happy about the disaster. But what had he done to make the tiny craft shipshape for a precarious sea? His fault was simply neglect. He had thought that the child, unhelped, unequipped, could make brave, sure conquest of the perilous paths of teen-aged experience.

What, moreover, had happened to the girl?

"Church might be okay for some kids," she now informed the minister, "but it's not for me. I guess it wasn't meant for me. Look what I am now—a bad kid!"

There comes a flood tide of interest in the higher currents. If the teen-ager loses that high, wonderful experience, it seems that the life is abandoned even as the mud flats after the flood tide has ebbed. There is no longer the vital urge to seek the spiritual harbors. And so with this one. Something sparkling, sweet, wistful died down deep within her. I could not find the magic again, nor could other interested Christian friends.

She was brought to juvenile court, a frightened child of thirteen years. Two sentences of hers stirred the judge, stirred the police, stirred her careless parents.

"Where are the boys?"

Parenthood could not be legitimately placed on any one of the four boys she had implicated. Neighbors hinted broadly that two married men were possibly involved in the scandal. The boys, guilty or not, were serving in the armed forces in faraway places.

"Where are the boys? Why aren't they here? Am I all to blame?"

There was another sharp and climactic moment.

The child had been given solemn, scathing advice. The responsibilities of parenthood had been drilled into her aching, bewildered head. She cried out in girlish manner to an awe-struck court:

"Why didn't somebody tell me these things?"

Somebody had reasoned, argued, pleaded with her father that an opportunity be granted the pretty, sparkling child one day a week to learn the ethic of Christ, the strong, courageous life, the radiant ideals of the Nazarene.

One fine Christian lady, present in court, said her heart ached for the scared, confused girl. The lady was thinking of a recent Sunday school lesson with its golden text, the words from a book of Moses: "Take this child . . . and nurse it [raise it] for me."

She said that the words throbbed in her mind as from the eternal Father and not simply as spoken by an Egyptian princess to a Hebrew mother. Later she narrated her experience to the girl's mother, whose single reaction was: "Bill and me, we did the best we could. Can't always pick a winner."

For days following the trial, the poor girl's image trembled in my consciousness, in contrasts—the shining angel of the graduation, the grim, grey-faced culprit of the court.

"I need her in the strawberry patch," a stubborn father had insisted.

The patch in question was not far from a fragrant woodlot where a cricket chirped his vespers of pure, melodic line, where a police car nosed up a grass-grown road among giant maples.

A few days after she had been committed to a state institution, to learn a few things, I spied a large, battered, green truck on the side of the hard-top road. Bill was packing berries, loading the boxes as he made ready for another day's business.

"How are you doing?" I asked him.

"Not so bad."

Was I remembering a tiny creature of God crammed with song and a bright, lovely girl sour on life and grown unmusical? Something, I know, was bothering me that hour, because I do not like to go along the roads lampooning everybody.

Nevertheless, I did have to say to Bill: "I hear it's been for you the biggest year ever—for *strawberries!*"

"Yes, Reverend, it has!" he triumphed, shoving a half-crate aboard a well-stacked vehicle. Then, seeming to read my mind, his face flushed, he choked and, jumping into the cab, the truck loaded with the beautiful berries, he went clattering on his way.

A younger girl was with him now.

Fight for a Life

I shall always see in my mind's eye a veteran of New England Congregationalism, dean emeritus of the Hartford Theological Seminary, Rockwell Harmon Potter, D.D., tramping along a solemn seminary corridor. His cane thumping in rhythm with the labored feet, he spotted my large, obvious shadow approaching.

I can hear him chuckling yet as I envision the portly, distinguished figure, his perennial hat not yet removed, as he ventured: "Well, if here isn't Phil Cleveland, the apostle of the ruins!"

He knew that I had accepted a call to a hurricane-smashed church in Canterbury, that I had reopened six closed churches in rural, northeastern Connecticut. His humor was even more obvious than my sharp shadow.

His words come back to me when I think of Elsie, the

Willimantic beauty, one of the prettiest blondes who ever sang in a church choir. They come back to me because in one ruined sanctuary we met; in a second crumbling shrine she found her haven of eternal peace.

The choir that welcomed me to Westminster Church in Canterbury boasted but seven members, ages twenty-one years to seventy-five.

Elsie was the living floral bouquet of the choir, always elegantly clothed in fascinating barrage of colors and styles. Her hats were prize offerings of Lady Fashion.

My first vivid recollection of her is a hat-wise one. Perhaps not so wise. One hat bragged a huge, flashy feather that turned a bewitching somersault over her alluring blonde curls. That feather dominated Elsie's hat; it dominated Elsie and the choir; and the real trouble with it was that it quite dominated the senior deacon's nose.

She was extremely fond of one genial bachelor-deacon, ecclesiastical society chairman, and she loved to tease the people she loved. She also felt that a deacon ought to pay heed to the preaching of the Holy Bible.

My sermons, like my articles, were too long, too wordy and preachy. And the deacon succumbed to all this and was prone to doze in the choir loft after the first thirty minutes.

When his head started to sag, Elsie always adjusted her hat. As the aging deacon, weary with milking cows, tending turkeys, gathering eggs, began nodding, Elsie's feather commenced its nodding.

As the deacon's face dropped, lower and lower, a great, grand, feathery plume dropped lower and lower; as it drooped it moved slightly, almost imperceptibly to the right. Elsie appeared to be meditative, devout; but the feather, not an ancient Pilgrim sexton's squirrel-tail, was touching the deacon's nose. Gently, gently the feather would reach an ample nostril and bend away. Half asleep, the deacon would raise a hairy hand to brush off the fly.

At frequent intervals he would hit harder. He would wake up, stare about him and later complain that the church screens weren't worth their salt. He never seemed to wonder why flies selected one nostril for adventure and never tried the other.

It is not always easy to preach Sunday sermons or for a choir to hold to church disciplines. One morning, consternation prevailed when the senior deacon cried aloud: "Drat that fly!" as he came awake. I will not describe the scene. Let this be sufficient: a solemn church delegation called during the week and on the next Lord's Day Elsie wore a new, handsome hat minus a somersaulting feather.

God was good to Elsie. Her resolute action one Sabbath morning saved my little boy's life from the ferocious dog. Five years later, to the amazement of all, a handsome boy entered their splendid home. Shall I ever forget the way Verne broke the news?

"Reverend, we've got you a new recruit for the church."

Elsie was transfigured beneath the magic wand of an adorable child. Three wonderful years brought astonishing rapture and blessing. And then, one day, visiting a relative's home, a kitchen stove exploded, a portion smashed into her chest—and in a few months cancer bumps were rising all over her body.

A long, bitter battle ensued—operation after operation, crisis after crisis, and the elegant lady found herself fighting the last grim enemy.

One day in the Norwich Hospital she made a confession.

Tapping a cigarette from a pack beside her bed, she declared: "Do you realize, Reverend, what a slave I've been to these things? Look at the size of this thing. See what helped to get me down! I used to hope my boy would act up in church so I could find an excuse to go outdoors and have my smoke. I couldn't even sit through a worship service without craving my cigarette. Silly, wasn't it? The doctor said that, being a chain-smoker, I have put up a poor fight."

She grabbed the small box and crumpled box and contents in a decisive palm. "Imagine a human being a slave to such a tiny thing!"

"Yes, for many they are coffin nails," I expressed simply.

Elsie found friends and good times in Westminster Church. But the miracle happened at the Second Congregational Church in East Haddam. The building had been sold to a Polish Catholic neighbor, after the handful holding on became discouraged. Hearing of its decline, I called on the Polish neighbor and bought back the church and reopened it. Here Elsie heard her last sermon.

A preacher from South Africa delivered a powerful message in the crumbling church one Sunday afternoon. Elsie attended, her right arm terribly swollen by cancer. It pained during service. The moment the benediction was pronounced she hurried from the edifice and inside her car.

"My arm is killing me!" she exploded. "Tear the sleeve—rip it open at the shoulder!" I followed her orders. However, the week following, she made a surprising statement.

"Something happened to me in that poor, old church last Sunday. I can't explain it. Peace, peace came to me. A year ago the thought of death would have driven me insane. Now all that panic has gone. The Christ you have preached became real to me as that man from South Africa told his experiences. I am not afraid of the future now. Reverend, something very wonderful has happened to me."

The weeks proved the truth of her confession. She commenced to read the Bible faithfully, to quote it, to ask questions about it.

"It gives me peace of mind," she sighed. "I've never known peace of mind. I've lived, had all kinds of fun, thrills, shows, excitements. But this new inner comfort, this peace of mind—it's the greatest thing I've ever known. Will you have a little prayer with me?"

Elsie and prayer! Elsie and the Bible!

Indeed, something very wonderful had happened in a sad, dilapidated church, even with pews ripped from wooden floors, the ceiling crumbling, foundations sagging, walls bulging. In a wreck of a rural sanctuary a dying woman had found the eternal sanctity. Indeed she did!

"Is the minister in?"

Calls, calls came, day after day, to read the Bible to Elsie, to pray when excruciating pain attacked her.

She wouldn't eat. Well, not until I came and ordered her husband and mother-in-law to bring in the dinner.

As we talked of faith, hope, and the everlasting mercy, Elsie would rise to a level of experience, interest, emotion, that gave her mastery over food. Many of us became aware of this miracle. Those who prepared meals waited for the pastor's afternoon call; it was time for lunch.

Poor me, I had no miracle bread to give, no secret of multiplication for loaves and fishes; but fish chowders, sandwiches, hot vegetables were devoured by a terribly sick woman as prayers were said, Biblical passages read, sentences of faith and courage spoken.

A minister without knowledge of applied psychology, spiritual therapy, Scriptural authority and an intense love for his people, will find it difficult to do real work in a dark room of slow death. This basic-maneuver lesson I learned in a pretty home where Killer Cancer raised his multiple heads.

One night Elsie had a terrible dream; she was still trembling in its boiling wake the next afternoon. As I took my accustomed chair in the upper room, at the bedside, she told the story.

"I was lying here last night when I found my peace of mind failing me. Oh, Reverend, I have lost it! I'm—afraid!"

"Tell me all about it."

Sitting bolt upright in bed, the once adorable lady, voice trembling, face dark with apprehension, the tenuous, musical voice commenced narration.

"I was lying here at midnight. My father was a rough man, a heavy drinker. He was sometimes a tyrant. He is dead. Last night he seemed alive. I heard him storming into the house, cursing, walking about. Where was Elsie? He shook the stairs as he climbed them." She panted for breath.

"An orange-yellow light shone under the door; it glared through the keyhole. It was terrible. He stumbled along the corridor; he laid hold on my bedroom door.

" 'I want to get in!' he yelled." Elsie reached for one of my hands.

"Reverend, it was awful! I lay so quiet, in a cold sweat head to foot, all shaky. When he found he couldn't break the lock, a long, sharp spear of light came at me through the keyhole. It grew longer, longer, until it touched my breast. The door creaked, groaned as that spear of orange-yellow light reached for my heart. But it only touched my flesh.

"I cried to God—the light faded—steps rushed out of the house—I awoke—my heart pounding like a sledge hammer. Oh, Reverend, why did that have to happen, to spoil my happiness? What did it mean?"

I faced a bitter crisis now as shepherd of a tortured lamb. Silently I asked God to help me interpret a strange, cryptic dream. I recalled that the eternal Father helped Joseph to understand dreams and gave Daniel insights of interpretation. My parents often sang a simple religious chorus: "The God who lived in Daniel's time is just the same today."

And I believe that I was somehow given a proper interpretation in a village cottage.

"Your father, Elsie, personified the evil power in this world that hurts dear, suffering people like you. That power tried to oppress you last night. What other power curses God and frightens helpless women?"

"That power tried to get in, to get at me," she chattered. "His lance pierced to my very flesh." Yes, to fearfully cut flesh, the breasts removed, cancerous. She was again bathed in the brackish waters of Lethe.

"But did that power get at you?" I insisted. "Did that power actually get at you?"

"No. He didn't. That's right."

"Do you know, Elsie, why the evil power could scare you, glance you, but could not really get at you?"

"Why couldn't he?"

"You have taken shelter in the Christian faith. Christ Himself said: 'I am the Door.' And that Door holds and will hold; it will forever hold. You often sing about the Friend we have in Jesus. The Friend will protect; that Door will hold."

Elsie broke instantly into convulsive sobbing; but there was relief in it, a great healing flood mingled with the outburst. In five minutes the stars again ascended into the dignity of her eyes. Once more the music trembled in the failing vocal organs of a still most gracious lady.

Another thing ought to be said.

One humid summer Sunday afternoon I dropped in between services. Elsie's lips were parched. She thirsted for orange juice.

"I couldn't hold it down if I swallowed it," she confessed. "For two weeks I have thrown it up a moment later. The spasms are terribly painful. Does anyone know what it is to be thirsty with so many good things to drink in the house and yet you dare not touch a single drop?"

"Perhaps you could take a glass of orange juice," I prompted.

"If I only could," she breathed. It sounded like prayer.

"It would only come up," Verne said sadly. "It would hurt her."

"Maybe one glass would stay down, Elsie, if you definitely asked your Friend, the Man of the Door, to keep it down."

Verne, a good man, flashed the strangest look my way as he left the sick room.

"I want you to bring Elsie a glass of orange juice," I called after him. He shoved the door open.

"Listen, Reverend, we've all tried a dozen times and Elsie is only let down again."

"Go ahead, hon," Elsie coaxed. "Do as he says."

When he returned with the glass I said to Elsie:

"Tell the good Nazarene, Doctor Jesus, that you'd appreciate it very much if you could quench your thirst without a violent reaction. Let us be simple and childlike. The kind Nazarene said we might ask a favor now and then. Ask and ye shall receive. Before you drink the juice, ask *Him* to keep it down."

She closed her eyes, bent her head and swallowed the entire contents of the glass. As she did I knelt and made a brief prayer. I felt impressed to do it: "Whatever powers are in the world, let us see if you are able to bring up that orange juice when we have invoked the kind Master to keep it down."

A full minute passed, two, three, five minutes. Husband, mother-in-law, pastor will not soon forget the indescribable look on a lady's grey face as, turning to Verne, she said: "*That glass* didn't come up, did it?"

I remained in the sickroom for two hours. That was a cool, refreshing drink for a dying lady on a fearfully muggy day.

Elsie dreamed one night that her boy had grown to manhood; he was a tall, handsome adult, graduating with high honors from a famous university, his father proud at his side.

"I wasn't there," she admitted. "But it's okay. Oh, my boy looked so wonderful! God is good."

At Easter time there was a brief resurgence of strength for Elsie. She felt so much better for a few days that she asked Verne to lift her from the bed. She was truly stronger. She wanted to arise and walk.

Smiling, vivacious, she placed exquisite slippers to the thick carpet. She held to Verne's strong arm and limping, holding it tightly, she walked as far as the large mirror. She gazed at a reflection.

"Hon, do I really look as bad as all that?" she exclaimed, weeping. "No, no, that can't be—me. Take me to the bed."

In three days the gracious, heroic lady had completed her earthly pilgrimage. The vast, wonderful peace had returned, the day following the mirror experience, and in its spell of comfort and beauty she sighed herself into her eternal rest. And a rural pastor returned to his daily work, to his sermons, his pulpit, to face a rural choir shorn of its brave and beautiful plumage.

The Hour That Changed My World

For two years, 1927-1929, I endeavored to raise my little parish family on the outskirts of New Haven. I was pastor of a small suburban church that was sold long ago to a business establishment. My first son, a three-year-old baby, fought for his life in the New Haven General Hospital, my wife giving him three transfusions of blood. A little girl entered the home —and bills and debts. The Sunday salary could not begin to cope with experience.

I was forced to work as salesman at a large furniture store. That, too, soon went under the hammer of defeat. Then I found work as salesman for a music store, member of a large New England chain. That store, ultimately, went the way of the church and the furniture house.

With mounting debts, a little, failing church, unable to make expenses though laboring seven days a week, I began to wonder if I was cut for ministerial cloth. Had I really chosen wisely in selecting the pulpit for my profession?

Having made a prolonged study of the piano in boyhood years, I proceeded to make a rather unusual sales record selling new and used instruments. The mother-store in Boston, scanning my good fortune, made overtures to me through the local manager. Would I care to go into special training and become a music manager? An attractive offer was made and I faced a crisis.

Let me report that the pulpit is my one supreme joy. To this day my "big thrill" is to open the sacred Scriptures and address a lively, eager congregation. I had also been reared in rock-ribbed Massachusetts and had been taught the practical religion of paying bills. While poised on the wings of momentous decision, I found an advertisement in the New Haven *Register*.

William Lyon Phelps was to speak at the Calvary Baptist Church on Sunday night. I had read many of the famous professor-author's volumes and articles. Could he preach a sermon? I wondered, and decided I must go. Fascinated by the thought I made my way to a thronged city church on a clear Sabbath eve to hear a message. I have not forgotten it. To this hour I recall the title and theme: "*The Cruel Promises of Jesus.*"

As Mr. Phelps dealt with his theme before a capacity audience he wove around me a spell of eloquence. I became aware, first, of well-selected words—perfect nouns, and explosive adjectives and phrases of exquisite description. I sensed a peculiar resonance of voice that suggested a continuous flow of melody. His articulation was exact; each vowel and consonant was given proper emphasis. He spoke as though every word in the English language reigned as king on a throne; there was beauty and polish in the flourish of every phrase.

He declared that Jesus won His youthful disciples because He challenged them—to hardship, struggle, difficulties; they would be summoned before magistrates and courts and would even face martyrdom championing a great cause.

He said that young men still wanted to live daringly and bravely, and cited as an example the fact that Admiral Richard E. Byrd always had to turn away an oversupply of volunteers for his hazardous Antarctic expeditions. Youth liked risks and dangers; youth liked to take stern chances, subduing continents and empires.

His voice increased in resonance and power as he said that with honest, cruel promises Jesus challenged fishermen and tax-collectors to win the hard heart of the world. He contrasted the early, embattled, heroic church with a smug and complacent faith in this modern world. He said that Christianity had lost its native air, its celestial fire and so it failed to appeal to red-blooded young people as it should.

I left that thronged sanctuary as a man walking in a dream. I had heard more gospel from a college professor than I would expect from most world-renowned preachers.

I must have a talk with Professor Phelps. That thought assaulted me over and over again; it survived a fitful sleep and came at me first thing in the morning.

Thursday I completed the decision and bent my steps in the direction of Yale University and asked the way to the office of William Lyon Phelps.

"Have you an appointment?" I was immediately asked.

"No."

"It would be impossible to see Mr. Phelps. He has an extremely crowded schedule today."

"It is urgent that I see him."

"Urgent?" echoed an attendant.

"I am a young minister. I have a wife and children. I am about to make a decision that will influence my entire life. I heard Professor Phelps preach Sunday night—and his sermon has brought me here."

"You are a pastor? A moment with him would mean so much? I don't know. Perhaps he would make an exception."

Fifteen minutes later I was ushered to an open door.

"Come in! I do have a few moments before lunch and will be happy to talk with you. My secretary has informed me that you were at Calvary Sunday night.

"Now sit down, young man, and relax and tell me precisely what is on your mind. What was it about the sermon that troubled you?" He slipped back into a rather large, golden-oak swivel chair, closed his eyes a moment, vaulted one agile leg and knee over the other and urged me to begin and to spare nothing; we were friends.

I narrated my experience as a salesman, covering the four points of the city selling pianos, renting them, merchandising radio combinations, renting used pianos to the Yale boys.

"You must most assuredly supplement your meagre pastoral stipend," he ventured decisively. "Of course this cramps your ministerial labor, your studies, your parish calling.

"But you realize that Christianity is no holiday excursion, as I said Sunday night. It calls on the red blood in us, on the resolute will, the flaming purpose. You have no doubt been long familiar with the cruel promises of Jesus."

I had no answer.

"Well, young man, I will tell you something."

Mr. Phelps paused a moment as though to concentrate on his attack. His eyes vibrated as brilliant prisms of light; his voice seemed reborn to youth and vigor. "I believe you are a salesman. Having talked with you, I shall agree with the wise men of Boston. You should be able to manage a store and sell good pianos."

"Then I should leave the church and train for a music store career?"

"I did not say that, young man. I said I believe you are a salesman. A line from Ralph Waldo Emerson is in my mind this instant. '*What you are . . . thunders so that I cannot hear what you say to the contrary.*'"

There was a prolonged pause and I was baffled, so the teacher continued.

"I mean, you are not selling me music; you are somehow selling me faith, hope, the church. Deep down you are a believer and should remain in the church!"

My whole body thrilled to his words, the purity and beauty of clean, inspired English. It swept over me like a spiritual shower-bath. Every nerve quivered.

"You . . . you talk like a real churchman," I stammered.

He chuckled and toyed with his glasses.

"Sometimes I think I may have missed my calling; but then, again, I believe I was made for books and classes and lectures. However, I certainly do not wish to see men who ought to be preaching the gospel just shoving rental pianos in and out of Yale dormitories. You should be giving the Lord full time, young man!"

"But, sir, I have told you—"

He cut me off with a new surge of enthusiasm.

"You have preached for a small denomination that does not possess adequate missionary funds. Now I think we can take care of that matter. I will send you to a wise man of Yale—my esteemed friend, Luther A. Weigle. He will advise you. Would you run over and see him?"

"Yes, sir."

"Good! Go, then, at once. I shall contact him. Mr. Weigle is a man of the church and he really has a gift in dealing with the problems of young preachers. I shall place you in good hands."

A few weeks later found me preaching in an historic, challenging Pilgrim sanctuary far up in the hills of eastern Connecticut.

Often I recalled on busy days, as I tramped the roads and visited the nearby cities and hospitals and prowled into the distant, hidden woodlands and looked up the needs and claims of folks here, there and everywhere, a twenty-minute talk with a world-celebrated English professor, teacher, author, who certainly gave me a lecture—and changed the world for me.

Violins and Harsh Voices

One day it was a lady's resonant, Jewish voice that inquired a bit timidly of my daughter:

"Is the minister in?"

"No. He's out on a sick call."

"He hasn't been ill, himself, has he?"

"No. Why do you ask?"

"Well, he hasn't been in to see David for a while and we thought he might be sick. Tell him to run in and see David when he comes to town. My husband is not well. He likes the minister. Will you have him run in—soon? Thank you. Sholom aleichem. Peace unto you."

Mrs. David R. Golden often chatted with my wife and my mother, but she called for me only this once.

The minister did see her husband on his next trip to a city

street, for town and country meet in this world and what God has joined together we can never put asunder.

But let us begin at the beginning. . . .

When I think of David Golden I think of a lilting rhyme, pieced together by Mary Kyle Dallas:

> He'd nothing but his violin,
> I'd nothing but my song;
> But we were wed when skies were blue
> And summer days were long.

It is certain that there were days when he had nothing but his violin; it is assured that there were days when I only had my song. We could not have nuptials, but we did discover strange, all but incredible harmonies, unities, yea, unities in disunities, as he mended violins and I voiced my unmarketable songs.

I can make no proper appraisal of this man—a short, plump Jew with tremendous head. His round, overdone head squatted over a plump, diminished body like a boulder sometimes tilts, holds by magic on the top of a tiny knoll. The arms were as much too long for the body's torso as the bowed legs were too short.

My brother was responsible for our acquaintance. He needed a violin repaired and I accompanied him to a narrow, cluttered, smoke-filled room in the rear of an imposing business block.

Sitting on a stool like a dwarf who could only thus reach a littered workbench I first spied little David, playing not a harp, but gluing bow-strings to the bow of a violin. A pot of glue was heated by an oil lamp; clamps, dozens of them, were stacked everywhere, bits of work-kits; violin-tops clamped to torsos, a cello held together by intricate scaffolding in a dingy corner, a viola lying broken on a side bench.

"Vat . . . you . . . vant?" A hoarse but penetrating voice invaded the resort of a thousand smells. Liquids, paints, glues, tobacco—what a bewildering congregation of odors! How could the man work in such a suffocating chamber?

I was not, of course, favorably impressed by the grotesque form in the rear chamber, by the tiny microbe-eyes that rushed like gnomes out of deep, dark caverns, ready to pounce upon me. His wildly gesticulating arms, giant arms sunk into dwarfed foundations, overlong, as though to atone for the ridiculous underpinning, did not favorably impress me.

It was a blessed relief to step again into the fresh air and clear out one's lungs.

I did begin, soon, to be impressed. That tiny chamber, a building's afterthought, proved to be too cramped for inundating business. David moved into a second room; expansions claimed a third room. Cellos, violas, violins from musicians moved from far distances into the still cluttered, almost impassable workrooms.

David opened a music store; he leased the entire first floor of the business block. Pianos, victrolas, radios, combinations, saxophones, drums, sheet music, records—he established a beautiful, shimmering house of music. Two boys and a girl were old enough now to wait on the trade. Purchasing sheet music and records, I turned often into the now elegant store. He liked having a minister running in to see him.

He always kept a door opened at the back of the store, leading to his main workroom; he must hear the floor traffic in case his children were preoccupied; he must be on instant call from them to close an impressive sale.

"Rev-rend," he used to suggest, "you play ze pi-a-no vile I

vorrk, eh vat?" I will not attempt to portray in English his broken, peculiar diction. The single sample must suffice. "Reverend, you play 'Kol Nidre,' 'Wings of Song' by Mendelssohn, play Schubert's 'Serenade.'"

Sometimes I sampled a Steinway, a Steinert grand, a Mason and Hamlin or Chickering upright, and often he sold the piano to a listening prospect. We became great friends.

In some respects he posited for me life's keenest challenges; he assaulted the Christian faith mercilessly; he leveled at me philosophical barrages that literally floored me, both in the music store and in the hot-glue workroom. He sensed how merciless his keen logic was, how forcible his keen-edged questions. Many a day hot, flaming words of his drove me home to examine again the chief tenets of the Christ, the policies of the church, as no seminary or college teacher ever did.

One sunny afternoon I was sampling a new baby grand in the store, improvising on a choice melody, Brahm's "Cradle Song," his son leaning on one end of the piano, his daughter on the other.

Through the open back door walked David, blowing cigarette smoke around him. Possibly it was the only pillar of cloud he believed in. Dark, sharp eyes snapped; a grey-white burst of unmanageable hair sprang from the huge bowl of a head. Thick lips opened to exhibit scraggly, nicotine-yellowed teeth, around which loomed a face with a week's growth of beard.

"Hah!" he grunted, moving close, puffing smoke, wickedly bright eyes grinning out at me from flourishing, ragged brows. "Hah, you should sell piano. You should never be Reverend. You should work for me; you make big success."

"Why do you think I could succeed?"

I stopped trying to rock an invisible infant across the rather remarkable black and white cradle of eighty-eight notes. I stopped fussing with the tender melody under the shock of attack. Once he hit with an argument there was no getting away for considerable time.

Surrounded by his curious children, grinning, arguing, David found what glory he found in life. This was the hour he sought, courted, wooed. Now I observed him again, the fat, plump body, the short, queer legs, the tremendous globe almost without neck with its fretwork of tangled grey-white hair, turning every-which-way. I could have laughed, but for the explosive power of his voice, the stinging impact of his words.

He shot to the piano; his fingers crashed to the ivories.

"Well, you hear piano, eh, what?

"You feel piano, eh, what?" He ran a hand along a highly polished side.

"You see piano, eh, what? You can smell piano, eh, what?" He rubbed a nose against the shiny, oiled finish. Then he attacked. Grinning from ear to ear, the yellowed teeth, each snag a spearpoint to impale the merciless logic, he challenged:

"Well, you can sell piano, because there *is* a piano; you can see, hear, touch, smell. But when you sell religion, what you sell? You sell God, truth, hope, love. What you sell? Can you see religion, can you smell it, touch it, hear it?" He thumped the keys violently.

"All the time I sell what is!" he fairly howled. Why, the dwarf seemed to climb a beanstalk that instant and his logic descended on me in overwhelming power. I was aware of this incredible transition. "All the time you sell what *ain't!*"

He laughed, a laugh in piecemeal, scattered into various small bits, yet the whole business strung together like beads, the bits of laughter of different keys, like a violin arpeggio.

"And if you can sell what ain't and make good living, how well you do if you work for me and sell what is!"

"Good, good, Papa!" chirped son and daughter as they saw he had harpooned me on the sharp yellow points of the remorseless logic.

Was I impressed?

David R. Golden, the diminutive Israelite, had delivered a dramatic lecture on the difficulty of proving the intangible as against the ease of declaring the tangible. Without time to study Hegel's logic, he often lunged into heavy, overwhelming dialectic.

Sometimes beaten, battered by him, I would studiously avoid him. He would ask my children why their father didn't run in to say hello. We have noted the time his good wife called the manse. One day he was working in a display window when his sharp eyes, suddenly lifted, spotted my shadow. He beckoned me indoors, nudged me into the smelly workroom.

"You reverends teach that God is love, do you not, eh, what?"

"We do."

"You say that Jewish teacher say that God is love, eh, what?"

"We do."

"You say this Jesus, this Christ is Jew, eh, what?"

"We do."

"This Jew teacher say God is love, eh, what? And he say we should love all people?" I wondered what he was driving at. It was plain he was driving somewhere.

"Yes, Jesus did say those things," I admitted.

"How is it then that you believe in Jewish teacher who say

God is love, and say we should love all people, yet you Christians hate the Jew, hate his own people? How can you Christions be square people? Tell me how?"

He lunged instantly into recitals of pogroms, persecutions, across the water and in New England, the indignities his wife had suffered, the scorn and contempt his children experienced from supposedly godly Americans. That harsh, steel-like, penetrating grin shall follow me into the tomb. Against my every attempt to prove him wrong, he marched out regiments of brutal, severe experiences.

There is no doubt in my mind that Nature had intended him to fill some distinguished chair of philosophy, to wear the cap and gown of remorseless logic, or to guide world conferences into paths of Experience and Reality. Never did any teacher so trouble me, upset nice theological applecarts, pour my nicely polished seminary teachings into the gutters, drive me home to read the Good Book again, to bend over the Sermon on the Mount, to hear his Countryman playing once more the far-off music of Galilee into my newly roused ears.

He was fearfully concerned when his eyes began to fail and only thick lenses permitted him to perform his mechanical feats of magic. His wife said that he became restless at home; he would go away for weeks at a time. Once he thought he might be falling in love again, this time with an exquisite, youthful violinist.

When he returned home sick, tired, worried, his faithful wife forgave everything; she hovered over him like a ministering angel, prayed to Elohim for his peace of mind and read him the Midrash for comfort; her strong, firm hands held together the empire he had built in order to cheer his last days.

Shall I narrate our final, pitched battle? I think I should.

Many encounters could be related, but the last one, just

before he died, to speak the language of the day, knocked me into the proverbial cocked hat!

That Friday afternoon he seemed almost wistful, searching. There was a faint gentleness to his bizarre gestures; about the corners of his thick lips played something that smoothed the harshness of the leering grin. To many ministerial meetings, conferences, seminars I have carried his last message. It is doing a posthumous work in the world and through it he, being dead, yet speaketh.

Seating himself among broken violins, battered cellos, damaged violas, the overrun glue pot offering incense to modify the nicotine aroma, he smoked less lustily, he talked less fiercely. He had been growing weaker. At times he labored to breathe.

"I need a master workman to put me in shape," he said, shrugging. "There are no clamps, no string, no pots of glue, to heal my broken instrument."

After a few general observations on the topics of the day, he spoke again with the impact that meant attack.

"I ask you one more thing." The eyes flashed out at me again, living fires fanning them. "Suppose we Jews, we want to join Christian Church. We call the congregation together. We decide to be Christian. We have good business if we are Christian; we have many friend. The wife, she have many friend; the children have many friend."

I commenced to speak. He touched my raised, sermonic arm; no, rather, he struck against it.

"You be still. I want to speak. We—all Jews—we decide to be Christian. But what Church be right Christian Church?" How he grinned, laughed that piecemeal laugh that tortured me. "Should Jew be Catholic Christian, Protestant Christian, Greek Orthodox Christian? Maybe he should be Baptist Christian, Methodist Christian, Church England Christian, even Pilgrim Christian. Well, what Church should Jew join? He not know. He poor Jew. He not know Christian way."

Once more I started to interpose; again a long arm stretched with vigor to my hand and he hit me a good one. He spoke petulantly; he was annoyed. He shook a little, shook all over when he became excited. The doctor had warned him about his heart. His hands were again moving in bizarre rhythm with the grotesque body.

"All Jew," he continued with increasing emotion, "all Jew ask Christian world to have conference. All Christian world will decide for poor Jew what is right Christian way so poor Jew be right Christian."

His powerful right arm hit my solar plexus a formidable blow; he repeated it.

"How long you think it be, Reverend, how long you think it be before Christian world decide for poor Jew what is right Church for him to join? You think, really, you think Jew *ever* find right Church to join?"

The music store has vanished now, with its clamps, the boiling glue, the skeletons of symphonic instruments. Others own the big building block; his children are scattered to the four winds. But I never pass along the pavement without strange stirrings inside me.

I think he could have lived forever and never have received an answer from me or from anyone else!

The Two Little Runaways

"Let me talk to the pastor. At once, please. This is an emergency."

Two teen-aged girls, sisters thirteen and sixteen, had run away from a state home twenty miles away and had last been seen heading in the direction of Canterbury. They had been missed at suppertime. Glancing at my watch I noticed that the hour was exactly eight-fifteen. It was a raw November night, a feeling of snow in the wind.

"Perhaps you can help us locate the girls before they get into serious trouble," begged the state official over the phone. "There is no telling what might happen to them."

"Where were they last seen, definitely?"

"We think in Danielson."

"I know Danielson fairly well."

"We know that, pastor. We'd appreciate anything you can do."

"What is it, Dad?" My own girl, fourteen, spare, graceful, spoke to me as I placed the phone on the receiver. "Is it anything serious?"

"It sure is."

Canterbury has a far, dismal fringe of French mill towns—Baltic, Occum, Jewett City, Wauregan, Danielson, Central Village, Putnam, Willimantic, Plainfield.

Having done some work for the Associated Press, to make an extra dollar, I knew social and moral conditions in these towns and villages. What pastor would not tremble for the security of two teen-aged girls, foot-loose and fancy-free, along the cold, lonely roads of deepening night in an area celebrated for moral laxity?

Moreover, I had served for nine years as chaplain of the Windham County Jail. The dangers of the area were obvious to me. And now two teen-aged sisters were wandering about, fugitives, somewhere in the villages or woodlands, engaged in perilous passage.

"God help me!" I prayed, backing the car into the road, "help me find those girls—before it is too late!"

Some years earlier figures had been published to the effect that the white slave traffic swallowed sixty-five thousand American girls every year. Recently the newspapers had carried the story of two sisters attacked, raped, slain in a western city.

My initial stop was Danielson. This low, flat community seemed to be sitting directly in the path of the girls. As news gatherer I had made some good contacts in the dingy borough. I made a dozen calls before I came up with anything.

A young lad, driving in from Moosup, said he was almost certain he noticed two girls a half mile the other side of town, hurrying along the edge of the Green Meadow Road.

"You are positive?" I insisted.

"Looked like two kids to me, just about the right ages. I should say. They were heading toward Wauregan. One was taller than the other, both skinny."

"Did one carry a suitcase?"

"I didn't see any suitcase."

Yes, I knew the twisting, serpentine road of the thick woodlands, a back road, Green Meadow Road. Two or three huge farms pierced its loneliness and monotony; a handful of houses were scattered at infrequent intervals along it. Said my grandmother once: "All life is so many ups and downs, more downs than ups." I will accept that as a description of the road in question.

Not a street lamp or light illumined the deep, black forest thickets for miles. Farms kept fierce watchdogs that barked menacingly from unseen haunts of inescapable night. God pity the poor girls if, to escape publicity and detection, they invaded the howling solitudes of Green Meadow Road on a cold, dreary night like this.

Thanking the lanky youth for his crumb of information, I left Railroad Square, shot past the uprearing white steeple of the Congregational Church, past the old high school, and soon invaded the mysterious privacies of a solemn road. Could the Genius which that tall, immaculate steeple symbolized aid me in finding two frightened, restless girls of today's confused schools? The thought whirred through my mind as the first length of the critical road rose into the yellow-white orbs of the headlights.

One mile up the road I had friends, due to a wedding a few years back. They owned a large, spreading farm and many head of cattle.

Had anyone heard anything about two little girls lost?

The genial lady of the house dialed a dozen phone numbers. No answer aided us in the least. Only the hired man's observation suggested a glimmer of hope.

"Two hours ago the dog was making a fearful rumpus," he confessed, "just like when he's got his nose to a woodchuck's hole or sniffed a rabbit's track. He wouldn't be after woodchucks or rabbits tonight. Now you don't figger he sniffed them girls off some place, do you?"

Five minutes later I was again exploring the hidden secrets of a grim, rural road, thin flakes of snow drifting down from the upper air, wind driving them about Green Meadow Road as though they might be themselves homeless fugitives. Silhouettes of the handful of dark houses loomed out of the gloom; dogs howled from tree-shaded yards of night. I traveled the length of the road to the tiny, squat, helter-skelter village, Wauregan.

Two places of business were still open. Nobody knew a thing about the runaway girls. I did not relish the remarks of two loud-voiced fellows as I made my brief statement. It wouldn't do far the fleeing teen-agers to meet up with these pool-players in their travels!

I glanced at my watch.

Nine-thirty.

In fifteen minutes I stopped at the Dragon Hotel, Moosup, made a quick run up to Sterling, then doubled back to Wauregan and along the cement highway to Central Village and Plainfield.

At a gas station in Plainfield, refueling, I exchanged words with a truck driver, Associated Transport. He said he was certain he had spotted, hours earlier, two girls, they could be thirteen and sixteen, warming themselves in a Danielson restaurant, on a back street I had missed.

Back to Danielson, to the fat, slap-happy proprietor of the restaurant.

"Sure—pop! Two girls did hit here, about seven o'clock. Got coffee and apple pie and chewing gum. Both of 'em seemed to be chilled to the bone. Weren't rigged for such a cold night. I made 'em stand about the stove a spell. Nice kids, too, the oldest one mighty pretty. Didn't want to talk none. The little one was coughin' plenty. I don't know, all of a sudden they were just gone, vamoosed. Why? Anythin' wrong?"

Once more I passed the thin, tapering Pilgrim spire, the imposing outlines of the old high school; again I approached the four corners with the overhead arc lamp and once more traveled Green Meadow Road, now in process of beautification. A lacy white carpet was being rolled by invisible hands up and down the climbing pathway. The hour was almost midnight.

What civic leader, state worker, pastor, father would not now be trembling in his shoes for the fugitives of a stormy Connecticut night? Somewhere, swallowed by these terrible, mystical miles of endless blackness were two no doubt frightened, frantic kids.

On to Wauregan!

On again to Moosup. Back across the bridge to East Brooklyn. And, finally, at two o'clock, once more searching the luring, inescapable haunts of the Green Meadow Road.

What is a hunch? Some time a very wise and erudite person will write a philosophy of hunches.

The police had been combing Putnam, Willimantic, Norwich. One rumor had located two girls in a Norwich theatre. While state police, sheriffs, state workers, the county detective, covered cities and boroughs, I recalled that there was a small, dirt road to the left that curved off the Green Meadow Road.

Could the girls, by any chance, have sighted it, have ventured into that most secret and isolated district?

In ten minutes I knocked at a humble cottage door. In twenty minutes, from a pay station along the highway, I had made contact with the proper authorities. And now to narrate a most bewildering story.

As an A. P. writer, a newspaper columnist, years earlier, I had met Mike McMann, an alcoholic. His favorite entertainment, indoor sport, business, recreation was—beer. He slept at home; he lived in the tavern. He would sit for hours and drain one tall glass of beer after another, smoking a special brand of spicy tobacco, rolling his own, between drinks.

Quiet-voiced, grey-headed, sloppily dressed, ex-soldier, existing on a good pension, Mike lived in a shack on the outskirts of the squat mill village.

"I'm my own best friend and I'm my own worst enemy," he told me once. I pitied him for his uselessness and apparent worthlessness to society. He never let anyone pry into a heavily guarded past that had no doubt been tragic.

Mike was picking his way home from the tavern, hitching along in the darkness. He said he could be blind and find his way home, he had traveled the beaten path so long. His always red, swollen, bleary eyes spotted two shivering outlines across the road. They tried to slip behind a tree.

"Heh, you!" Mike called to them. "What's goin' on here this time o' night? Come over here!"

He mumbled later over a bottle of beer that he didn't know what came over him; he seemed to know just what to say, just what to do. He had surprised himself.

The girls had tried to deceive Mike about their homes, their reasons for being on the road. Mike McMann had been around, he said; he knew a thing or two.

"You kids is about dragged out, frozen; you'll get pneumonia. I know you're not streakin' it for home, not the way you're actin' up. You two is in trouble!"

Mike has a mild, musical voice. He was once a handsome, engaging fellow.

"I'm an old duffer, kids. I wouldn't hurt a hair o' your heads. You'd best trot along with me. You're chilled to the spine. I'll fix you up some hot soup, brew a mite o' coffee, prod the fire. We'll get things straightened out—later."

Trembling, chilled, scared to death, the two sisters had followed Mike to his shack, had swallowed the hot soup; both had tumbled, clothed, into his bed.

When I arrived he was sitting in the tiny kitchen over a bottle of beer wondering what to do, wrinkling his brows over the knotty problem. The dear, sleeping girls, out like a light, as he informed me, had unburdened their hearts to him. It was my turn now to be truly staggered.

"Reverend," he said to me, "you know why them girls is runnin' away? They're good kids. I knew it; they're wonderful kids. They're runnin' away to preserve their decency."

"What do you mean?"

"Those kids want to keep clean!"

"What?"

"Yes, in the state home where they were livin', a man had been forcin' his attentions on them kids. He was gettin' fresh, mighty fresh, I call it. He's gonna get the works, that guy. Them kids is good kids."

What! Mike McMann a father-confessor, friend of youth, determining that justice must be meted out in this world? I just couldn't believe my ears. Suddenly a man I had pitied, scorned, became indeed—a wonderful guy.

The story was a true one. Soon Connecticut rocked in the throes of a storm more violent than a November night. More than one official person tested the strength of prison bars; the state ordered a housecleaning. Two fugitive girls, cowering from the dense shadows of a snow-swirling night, brought a new, glorious day to many children in New England.

Little did I dream, as I rushed back and forth across the eerie landscape of a rural evening, that two teen-aged sisters, going on before, were preparing my state for a lovely snatch of song, that beautiful ballad: "Dear Heart, the world is waiting for the sunrise."

And how I thank my God that the lone, sad pilgrim of the bleak night and the bleak house was none other than a man who in bitter crisis-hour proved himself a man, yea, more than a man—a gentleman!

I have never ceased to pray that he too will find shelter, peace, and understanding when he goes forth into the vast, impenetrable Dark.

The Salvage of Youth

My experiences with Connecticut churches were not promising. One, in New Haven, became a laundry in later years. The Brooklyn Trinitarian Congregational Church was demolished by the '38 hurricane. The Canterbury sanctuary was unmercifully beaten by the same storm.

Before the '38 hurricane hit Brooklyn, two most astonishing men hit town one clear Sabbath morning: Roger W. Babson, statistician, and William Hotchkin, the Boston broker.

Some time earlier I had inaugurated the chaplaincy at the Babson Institute, Wellesley, Massachusetts, on a part-time plan.

Mr. Babson had written me, asking for an interview. Yes, the minister was in and available for conference. Months of exciting and profitable experience followed. Mr. Babson knew that friendship is not a one-way street. I had gone to the Bay State; he would visit in Connecticut.

One portentous Sabbath, an imposing limousine added its brilliant length to the roadside and two striking strangers moved into rear pews. I knew Mr. Babson; I did not know his companion.

The old church owned a tremendous box of a pipe organ, of unsightly pipes and clashing colors, but Mabel Leavens, the widow-organist, could do anything with it, provided she was allowed to. You see, it was wind-blown by hand. She performed the hymns with amazing power if the girl behind the long, brown curtain gave her the power. The heirloom of an organ was at first fed by manpower, and such power failing, girlpower prevailed. Ellen Ingalls, a girl of fourteen, pumped the old ark. Sitting on a narrow chair she propelled a thick, wooden lever up and down with vigor. If she grew tired or dozed, the poor old organ would wheeze, choke and with most fearful moanings give up the musical ghost!

While the hymn before the sermon was stirring the audience, the huge, impressive antique commenced to groan, wheeze and snuff itself out. Mabel's powerful fingers thumped impotent keys.

What to do? Slide along the bench, lurch to the right and whisper, good and loud: "Pump, for pity's sake pump!"

Suddenly old vocal cords came alive; there was a furious, invisible clamor, wood banging on wood, the organ shook, trembled into song. With a climactic rush, wind poured into all the tremendous pipes and now the whole edifice quivered in musical impact.

Roger had observed the incredible phenomenon and his eyes surmised the invisible gyrations of the musical x-y line. What was going on behind the drawn curtain?

The moment the benediction was given he strode up the carpeted aisle. He cut an impressive figure, moustache, goatee and all, and his voice boomed in my ear: "Cleveland, who's back there? I want to meet the Invisible. Who's pumping the old ark?"

As I thrust open the curtain a tall, lovely girl stepped to the platform.

Roger held out a hand. "I want to meet the power behind the *tone!*" he declared with resounding voice. His breezy, whole-souled humanism was a splendid thing to see. "I did not expect to find the invisible power so young and attractive!"

Roger revealed his true self after church, congratulating one who was so essential to divine service. I shall never forget a rural girl's simple rapture in the presence of a great man!

Mr. Babson introduced his companion to the girl, to me, to my wife. It was my first sight of the handsome man of State Street, Boston, William Hotchkin. A more cultured man I have never met. He spoke to me, his words gentle and polished: "I have purchased the famous Wolf Den Farm in Pomfret, near the site where Old Put [Israel Putnam] cornered and killed that old she-wolf. Mrs. Hotchkin and Mrs. Babson would enjoy having you and your wife for dinner today. Could you come to our home in another hour?"

What a delightful place! What a charming hostess! What a thoroughly enjoyable time!

Roger had to leave for Wellesley shortly after dinner. A servant brought two bags and placed them in the trunk of his car. Roger turned to his wife and smiled. "See the initials on those bags?" He pointed. "They are G. K. B. One might think they stand for Grace K. Babson. But what do you suppose they really mean? When anyone asks my wife, she always answers: 'Grace Knows Best.' However, when a preacher asks her what the letters mean, she always replies: 'God Knows Best.' " I shall never forget the playful lights that mingled with his words or the sweet, amused expression of his congenial wife.

I wondered what kind, invisible Power other than music had guided the feet of Boston's expert financier to the old Pilgrim shrine that Sunday. Two weeks later the logic of events revealed itself.

A Portuguese lad, seventeen, called Chops, knocked on the back door of the manse at dusk. To Priscilla he said:

"Is your father around? I got to see him."

"Yes, he is in."

Chops was plump. He said that his father, looking on him in the cradle, exclaimed: "What a pair of chops for a kid!" The lampoon stuck. The heavily built lad, dark-skinned, poorly educated, worked for an aged spinster on a battered farm, his pay board and room.

Chops whispered to me in the kitchen: "We got to be alone." He labored to speak. "I don't want nobody around."

In the study he made a sad confession.

Older boys had challenged him to break open and enter a summer home. They had stolen and had pawned objects. The police had traced the vandalism. The owner of the place offered to settle for one hundred dollars. The judge would place Chops on probation if the money could be raised. But where could an orphan, a child who had never known the luxury of parents, find two fifty-dollar bills?

"I know I done wrong. I shouldn'ta done what the big kids told me to. And who'd loan the likes o' me a hundred bucks?"

"You're worth it, Chops," I informed him. While talking I thought of a recent Sabbath and a man who had said he had tried to be a big brother to city kids.

"I think I know where we can raise the money," I encouraged.

"Who'd do it—*who?*"

"Never mind now, Chops."

"Gotta have a hundred bucks by next week."

"I think we can have them."

A letter to Mr. William Hotchkin went forward in the morning mail. A check for one hundred dollars came back at once. I read his note: "You see that the check is made out to you. The boy's name will not even be recorded in the issuance of the check. Hand the lad the money as a loan. I have an idea."

Chops couldn't believe his eyes when he held ten crisp bills in his hand. The dour, aloof boy commenced to attend church and to mingle with a better class of young people. Within a month Mr. Hotchkin called at the manse.

"Send the lad to my farm. He can work out the loan week ends. Perhaps I can help him. He has never had any kind of parental training. This relationship will be good, I think, for both of us. Send him up to Wolf Den Farm. Perhaps we can make his capital stock worth something and one day put it on the market of good citizenship. Who knows what we might do with that boy?"

Chops was bewitched by the kind of man he worked for every week end. A shrewd Bostonian discovered he had actually made an excellent investment. Chops' value kept rising, week by week, until his benefactor was amazed.

Mr. Hotchkin became so fascinated with reclamation work that he mailed the warden of the Windham County Jail, Brooklyn, Connecticut, a check for twenty-five dollars. The jail officials were so thrilled by a Boston bequeathal that the check was framed and fixed to the office wall for many months.

In my scrapbook I keep some treasured pages of correspondence from a man of genius, a man of means. Few suspect that in a poor boy's hour of harsh crisis, the Boston broker became "the friend that sticketh closer than a brother."

Mr. and Mrs. Hotchkin have departed this earthly life. Long ago the vast, immeasurable things of Time and Space engulfed the boy named Chops. A hurricane destroyed even the church they attended. The minister has moved out of his beloved New England. And yet, I never drive through Brooklyn, Connecticut, without seeing in clearest memory a most charming and courteous Bostonian placing a hand on an orphan's shoulder and bidding him to lay hold of Life: "Son, the world is yours if you know how to make it yours!"

Words like those never die, nor do their magic and beauty ever fade away!

Finnish Fracas

"Heh, man, you crazy!"

A shout of warning from the rear chicken coops came too late.

"Go back!"

There was no turning back. A huge body, black and grey, was almost at my feet, arrowing through the grass, rattling the steel wire overhead, the chain at his neck.

What to do?

I could not escape him, hurrying forward or backward, and so I braced for the shock. Doing this, my feet found a clump of soft, wet grass and, fortunately for me, I lost my footing. The exact moment the dog leaped, a heavier and more formidable body leaped at him, or rather, flung its considerable weight at his face.

The thing happened so suddenly! I can scarcely recall the

minute details or place them in sequence. I knew that by some marvelous piece of luck I fell on that vociferous creature and struck him to the ground; in fact, my entire two hundred pounds landed on his stomach and for an instant that canine was literally knocked out.

Part Russian wolfhound and great Dane, he had posed a serious threat. I scrambled to my feet as a Finnish farmer dashed down a slope and grabbed the dog by the neck as, snarling, hair bristling, he shook himself and snapped to his feet.

"You man, you crazy! You not see dog?" a stern, scolding voice demanded.

"I thought he was chained to the side of the cottage, over by the dog house."

"You not see heavy wire that run from cottage across yard to shed?"

"No."

Indeed I hadn't. Overarching trees all but concealed the long wire, the sun having dipped westward behind the chicken coops.

"Selim, what happen? Any trouble?"

A buxom, lively lady ran down the slope from a rear coop.

"Not much trouble. But man, he crazy; he want to lose big hunk of him!"

The powerfully built, platinum blonde, square-headed Finnish farmer kicked the now cowering creature toward the doghouse.

"Per-ru, bad boy! Go to bed!" he commanded as the vociferous canine, subdued, with a whining cry dashed to his tiny domicile and vanished.

"Per-ru?" I inquired. I believe he said it was the Finnish

word for dog. A rural canine had nearly finished my small son's career; it was not pleasant to realize that another could have concluded mine.

The deep-blue eyes searched me, head to toe, as I retrieved my black hat from the wet grass and brushed my trousers.

"Who you be? You—salesman? We not be much for salesman."

"I am the preacher on the hill."

"You Meester Clev-e-land?" he queried, now really giving me the once over and not lightly. "You priest—help find girls that run from state home? You priest call on Russian farmer and say, 'Tovarich'?"

"That's right."

He grinned at the smiling woman, scarf wound about her head, red and white apron tied snugly about her. She was also studying me with penetrating gaze, two long, yellowish pigtails dangling down her back.

"Lempi, this—priest. We have coffee—with him. You brush off clothes. We all go to house." He flashed a threatening eye toward a dark snout sticking from the doghouse.

"Per-ru, very bad boy!" he scolded. With one bark of confession the black snout disappeared.

"You—very strange priest," he said to me in the pretty, colorful kitchen over Finnish cake and coffee. "You not see wire. You make battle with big, bad Per-ru. You fight. You kay-o big fighter. You make him look foolish. You very strange priest."

The childlike simplicity of the Finns always impresses me, the sincerity of their judgments, the unspoiled youthfulness of their emotions, the utter honesty of their statements.

"Do you two ever get out to church?" I ventured as we finished a light lunch.

"We too busy," Selim acknowledged. "Many broiler, layer, capon, caponette. Market not good. We work hard. Take all time we have to pay bill."

"Priest like chicken for pot on Sunday?" the now talkative wife suggested. "We have chicken just right for stew."

"Yes," added Selim, rising from table. "Lempi pick out good, fat chicken. It is Thursday. You go home, kill chicken, put in freezer; be just right for dinner Sunday."

"I—I couldn't kill a chicken," I confessed. "Tried it once—shoved its head under the axe on the chopping block; never again."

With a grin he turned to his wife. "Lempi, you bleed chicken, get water pail, pluck. We kill chicken. Priest not have to dirty hands."

"It's not that," I explained. "It just upsets me to kill anything."

"You—jumpy—to prepare chicken—for stew?" he questioned. "Yes, I say you sure be one very strange priest—one very strange priest."

I did enjoy an excellent chicken dinner on Sunday and thanked God for the edible gift and did not lay eyes on the hard-working farmer and his wife until the following year.

At a Finnish wedding I shook hands again with Selim and Lempi. They observed that I loitered about the box of soft drinks while the other males indulged in beer and wine.

"All you drink is that—fizz?" Selim ventured. "No bottle of beer?"

"Ginger ale is my drink."

"Huh!" he grunted, grimacing. "I say once more you very strange priest. Here you can drink all beer, all wine you like, and you drink that fizz!"

When he watched me swinging the handsome Finnish children in a sunny yard, whirling them in giant circles under elms and maples until children and parson were alike dizzy, he approached.

"How you find time—for that?" he asked. "You so busy with churches. I hear you preach in three. How you find time to be kid once more?" Shaking his head, flashing a queer, mystified look upon Lempi, he said goodbye to me, again remarking that Connecticut had a most strange parson on its hands.

Then the 1938 hurricane rushed, not a vociferous canine, but a roaring killer, on the tiny town of Brooklyn. Overnight a trim, neat area became a logging camp of fallen, stacked timber. One twisting, violent hurricane-center reached for the church steeple, wrenched it from its base like a boy twists paper from his favorite candy. Yellow sea-sediment, blown a hundred miles from the Atlantic, covered the clapboards of the terribly hurt church.

The wind's fist wrenched off that heavy steeple, lifted it free in a black whirlpool of air and let it drop, weather vane down, through the roof, through the floor. The spire smashed into the ground beside the furnace in the cellar.

The church folks decided to reopen a nearby, closed edifice and tear down the beautiful old Congregational sanctuary. I fought with everything I had to save an historic building where my wife worshiped and my children had been dedicated to the high, white ideals. I have fought many a battle and suffered many defeats. Once more I lost.

Finally the church folks asked a Moosup wrecking company to remove the tremendous, imposing structure looming beside General Israel Putnam's magnificent monument and Mrs. Theodore Roosevelt's summer home.

It seemed to me that poetic lines from my native countryman, Oliver Wendell Holmes, were ringing in my ears:

Ay, tear her tattered ensign down!
Long has it waved on high,
And many an eye has danced to see
That banner in the sky. . . .

It seemed I could almost feel the pain as that lordly old structure stiffened against the Norwich winch that strained, a strong, modern Samson, against the four great white pillars that had supported a noble head high over good and evil things for many a year.

"Everything that goes up has to come down, sooner or later." We had to deal with such flippancies in an hour of crisis.

The graceful, towering steeple of the Danielson Congregational Church had crashed on the highway; the Lebanon sanctuary was split in two; the Jewett City church was demolished. But I have never been able to reconcile myself to the deathbed scenes of Brooklyn's impressive landmark.

One cold, windy November Sunday morning I started for the tiny chapel that remained unhurt beside the huge edifice, a small square building where we served church suppers and the ladies held sales. We were temporarily holding services in it.

Ironically enough I had selected for theme the permanence and power of the Christian Church. My text? "These things write I unto thee . . . that thou mayest know how thou oughtest to behave thyself in the house of God, which is the church of the living God, the pillar and ground of the truth" (Timothy 3:14,15).

Fifteen minutes before Sunday school, the Norwich winch

was flinging its metallic strength against four magnificent pillars. The wooden-pegged building, powerfully built, groaned, withstanding this secular attack on a sacred day.

Coming down the road I heard the unmerciful racket, spied the workmen, remembered a sermon. What psychology! While I proclaimed the church the permanent dwelling of truth and right, the Norwich winch would be tearing the pillars from the roof and the secure ground!

I . . . got . . . mad.

Yes, let us confess to human frailty and to a certain New England individualism. Mother brought me up with this sentence: "Tell the truth and shame the devil." I bent into the chill November wind and hurried to the busy foreman.

"What are you doing?" I demanded.

"Our business. We just rented that winch, so much a day. The quicker the structure falls, the sooner we can take the winch back."

"You were hired to tear the church apart on the Lord's Day?"

"No! But the quicker the old ark crumbles, the better!"

"Listen, you!" I cried. "Kids are due here any minute. I'm not going to have them see this church going down at church time. What kind of brains have we got to sell them the idea of church while the church topples to the ground?"

"I'm no churchman. What does it mean to me?"

"You just get out of here!" I roared. "I'll not have this church pulled apart Sunday morning while I'm preaching. What do you think we are? Nitwits, numbskulls and neurotics?"

He glared at me and said some sharp things, which I have forgotten.

"I'll call the state police!" I threatened.

"On what charge?"

"Disturbing the peace, profaning the Sabbath!"

His face went white and as I spoke a trim little auto, just passing by, stopped.

"Okay!" boomed an irate foreman. "But you'll have to pay for the day's work just the same!"

"Stop this racket at once!" I ordered.

A young, resolute Finn stepped from the car, sized me up, my red face, my eyes of flame, I suppose. It was Selim.

"You sure be very strange priest. You crush dog. Now you crush workingman. You swing children, drink fizz; but you fight, huh, priest? I not think you really know how to fight, just scare Per-ru! Wait till I say to Lempi what I see, what I hear! You like church like I like chicken coop!"

The following Lord's Day the pillars were no longer visible beside the highway; only the church walls were standing; but, to my amazement, Selim and Lempi entered the tiny chapel, just in time for the sermon. I could scarcely believe this new development beside the hurricane ruin.

Said Selim later: "I wonder what very strange priest say to people. Can he scare people like he scare dog? Can he talk to people like he talk to boss?"

The Sunday the church shook in the claws of the winch, threatening to collapse, a strong, skeptical youth found his own ground of faith and hope and soon two wonderful young people turned their hearts simply and like little children toward the Eternal Shelter.

Last Call to a Family

I would rather preach than eat. To break the bread of life to an eager audience is my chief joy in this surprising world. For me, the preparation of a sermon calls for intense study, hard application, exegesis, illustration, argument, inspiration and consummate artistry.

Now just suppose a man has worked hard, completing what he considers to be a good, timely message, adds the finishing touches only to feel, at the last minute, that he hasn't his sermon?

I sat down Saturday morning to meditate on Sunday's message, already completed, a message on hope and vision, when that sermon went as flat and became as unpalatable as yesterday's pancake.

Suddenly I realized that there wasn't anything in it for the people. Scanning the typed pages, now "nothing but leaves," lifeless, decaying autumn leaves at that, another invisible wind stirred through the study.

You ought to preach a sermon on the Christian home. It has been considerable time since you delivered a message on Christ in the home. The idea of children seized me with a strange, challenging impact. *How little children need the love and tender care of Christian parents! Do children have a fair chance in life who do not sense the charm, the beauty of Christ in their parents, in the devotions of the home, in the everyday experiences of daily life?*

This thought came to me out of somewhere, blowing into the inner laboratories, stirring the hidden vitalities. I recalled the radiant Christian atmosphere of my boyhood Bay State home. Father and Mother awoke on clear Sabbath mornings to play and sing the soulful hymns of faith. The family altar was used in times of stress and strain. The Bible always glimmered beneath the lampshade.

Yes, the text, theme, the logical development of theme, arguments, warnings, challenges, illustrations, applications—that entire sermon came to me like Peter's sheet let down from an unexpected height. And, as happens with my best sermons, the moving, scintillating thing seemed to write itself.

A lively youngster, who frequently whistled in school, was reprimanded by the teacher. He replied: "I can't help it! It whistles itself!" Sermons that just come—well, these are the sermons that go places!

I was amazed at the last-minute Saturday message, "Christ in the Home," at its apparent logic, freshness, challenge. I knew it would be the next day's offering and it was. Not until ready to stand and deliver it, preliminaries all nicely out of the way, did I observe a strange family moving up the east aisle, slipping into a side pew. Four of these six latecomers were small children, three girls, one boy. It was not long before I became aware of the intense interest of the lady. She had slumped in the pew; she was now becoming alert, her body stiffening, straightening. The eyes grew brighter, the face moved forward in expectancy.

Many preachers are aware of particular people in their congregations, people who are all ears to a message; they sense certain thirsty souls in the sanctuary drinking in the pulpit showers. This lady could not have been more than thirty-five. She stood out among a hundred communicants as a detached point of vision, a shining target for the gospel marksman. She made herself the perfect target, her eyes riveted upon the altar, her full, round face "fair as the moon," rapt, wistful. As I preached, noticing the three girls, the boy, I became convinced that this sermon had been specifically designed for them.

Following the benediction the family lingered on the lawn at the edge of the church entrance. When I stepped to the ground the lady was at my side, four children clinging to her, a lean, quiet man just behind. She extended a tapering, beautiful white arm and glove. She had been waiting outside some twenty minutes as two deacons inside mentioned matters of urgent business.

"I want to thank you, pastor, for that message."

Her voice was soft, quietly musical as a May night. The lips, smiling, could enchant the universe. She was indeed a vision of delight. One sensed reality in her voice, a great seriousness in the overtones.

"It was exactly what I needed, what Al needs, what we all need, especially the little ones!"

Her arms were flung about four wiggling, gayly colored forms swaying about the orchid dress.

"Wasn't that a sermon, Al?" she said, turning back to her husband who grinned and nodded.

"Would it be asking too much, pastor, to call on us this week? I know you are a busy man. But it is quite urgent. Do you think you could call—soon?"

"Where do you live?"

"The other side of Willimantic." She gave explicit directions.

"I do not wish to appear dramatic, but it would mean a great deal to have you call." She lowered the musical voice to the merest whisper as she stepped closer. "I really need—help. Can you come?"

"I will be over this week without fail."

"Thank you, oh, so much!"

I watched six strangers, a little family that had filled a Pilgrim pew, aisle to wall, moving toward a parked car.

Thursday afternoon I followed directions to a handsome new house in a housing development. The lady of white-birch skin, billowing blonde hair tied with flaming, scarlet ribbon, answered the door and thrust forth a hand.

"I thought you might call today, it is such a glorious day! Do come in!"

The oldest girl was in school. Two girls and a boy were having their afternoon naps. I found myself in an elegant room, splendid shining things everywhere, original oils on the walls, an expensive television-phonograph in one corner, a baby grand in another.

"I must tell you about everything, pastor. I thought you might have to face a crisis when you called this week. But you don't! There isn't any crisis. Oh, it is truly wonderful!"

"Would you mind letting me in on the secret?" I suggested, having a hunch that she might be on the verge of delivering a sermon herself.

She laughed a rollicking laugh, tuneful, coloratura-laughter;

she seemed gliding up and down a whole octave when she laughed. It was joy to listen.

"Well, pastor, last week I took out my first divorce papers. I left him once—before. This time I was determined to separate from him, for good. He was getting on my nerves. I had got on his. He works days. I have been working nights. I didn't have to work. But why stay home and fight? We began to grow apart while he was in the army. I followed him around the world in army camps, toting babies. He began to go his way; I commenced to go mine."

"You both began to be interested in others?" I interrupted.

"No, pastor, nothing like that. I just began to dislike Al, to hold him off when he came near, to build a wall between us. He commenced living to himself. When I said we were poor at the role of hypocrite, if we couldn't love each other we should separate, he told me to use my own judgment.

"Last week I began divorce proceedings in earnest.

"A man I ride to work with, a Boy Scout commissioner who attends your church, found out my plans and asked me if I had given God a chance." She searched my eyes deeply. "His words bothered me. Had I given God a chance? He said I ought to go to church once, at least once, before making further plans. He kept at me all last week."

I suggested a man's name. The lady nodded.

"He was supposed to pick us up Sunday morning, but his little boy became ill in the night. There we were, the six of us, all dressed up and nowhere to go! What should we do? I said we would go to church just the same." She grinned an almost unpardonable grin as she confessed: "We arrived too late for the collection."

Perhaps she wasn't preaching, but an eager, earnest lady

had captured a preacher in the sparkling charm of a beautiful recital.

Returning home after service she became unusually aware of the children, she said. Had she realized before what the children meant to her and what she must mean to them? And were they not her children because she had vitally loved one man in all the world?

"Something happened to me between your church and my house," she declared.

Arriving home she decided against the regular Sunday dinner.

"Let's pack a picnic lunch, Al, and go to the lake. You like boating. Let's go boating!"

Lunch was hastily packed, and bathing suits, caps, water balloons, a floating ball filled the trunk.

Arlene and Al became two silly, romantic things all over again, swimming, diving, boating, eating hot dogs, ice cream cones, playing with the children, strolling in the land of the sky-blue water.

"By sunset I was in his arms," she confided. "I will stay there this time. I have stopped working nights. I'm going to learn to be a first-class wife and mother. I owe that to Al and the children."

She whisked to her feet and reached for my hand. How childlike she really was!

"See what I have put up over the fireplace in the next room." In a moment she pointed to a colorful wall motto.

CHRIST IS THE HEAD OF THIS HOUSE
THE UNSEEN GUEST AT EVERY MEAL
THE SILENT LISTENER TO EVERY CONVERSATION

"Oh, it's so wonderful!" she triumphed. "Through the church we have found our home, our children, our love again!"

"And a sermon did all that?" I asked simply.

"No," she replied with a most bewitching toss of the billowing hair, with a most entrancing lift to the blue eyes, "the sermon didn't really bring us together. It was what the sermon pointed out," she owned, frankly, beautifully.

"And that was—"

"The children!" she exclaimed. "Excuse me! I hear them upstairs. It is time they got up, time for the oldest girl to get home from school. They will want to see you."

In another year a fifth child tiptoed into that shining home, the blonde baby, with fairylike hair, rose-petal cheeks, a sweet oval face also fair as the moon, indeed the love child! Heaven rewarded their heroic resolve with a child exquisite enough to be divine.

These people are leaders today in my son's Connecticut church, close to the lake of the fragrant water lilies where one critical Sunday afternoon they washed souls and bodies of pride and prejudice and, newly baptized, started to live again.

A Scotsman Surrenders

There is no need to make a long story of Sandy, the proverbial Scotsman.

In this instance the aging bachelor was well named. His complexion was sandy; his thinning hair was sandy; his disposition was a mite sandy; his blue eyes blended nicely with the expanse of sand.

My first sight of him was in the grassy, bumpy cemetery lot at the rear of the church. Working about the church lawn, I heard a yell from the graveyard and dashed through an open iron fence to spot a little, resolute shadow pounding the turf with a cane.

"He got away!" cried a sharp, sandy voice. "He was a striped adder. The gravestone here had toppled. I picked it up when that snake slithered from the shadow. They say you might as well kill a man as scare him to death! And I'm to be buried in the next lot—beside mother."

"Do I know you?" I inquired.

"I'm Sandy McPherson. I live a mile down the Hampton Road." He described his dwelling.

"I called twice. Nobody seemed to be around."

"I was probably in the chicken coop. Call again some time. You must be the new minister."

"That's right. Have I ever seen you in church?"

"No. I'm retired. I'm retiring from the chicken business. Years ago I retired from real estate. I've retired from a judgeship. I'm retired from church."

"Should you ever retire from divine worship?"

"I'm Episcopal. Used to sing in the boy's choir in Trinity Episcopal, Brooklyn, New York. There are no Episcopal churches in this vicinity. I stay home now. I read the New York papers on Sunday."

It was like pulling the proverbial hens' teeth to pull Sandy out to the local congregation. He lived "all by his lonesome," as he said. His favorite tune was an old Fred Astaire number: "I'll go my way by myself."

"You never married?" I asked him one day.

"Why should I marry? A woman cooks. I cook. A woman washes clothes. I wash them. A woman irons clothes. I can iron. A woman cleans house. Mine is clean. But a woman can talk back and an empty house can't, now can it? And one can live cheaper than two. If I had to buy victuals and clothes for two, and Easter bonnets, my pension wouldn't hold out!"

The blue eyes had mischievous spear-points of light glowing in them. His resonant voice suggested a bit of sand and grit. His fingers talked in rhythm with words.

Sandy continued: "In fact, dominie, one reason I quit church was because some gay, saucy widow was always flinging herself in the aisle between me and the door. Couldn't keep my thoughts on the ritual. So I stay home with the news!"

Yes, I often caught Sandy preparing a lonely supper, doing the weekly washing, reading the city papers beneath a tremendous lampshade.

He was most punctilious and precise about things. He kept a prim, shiny Model T in his barn. Every Friday morning he went shopping to Plainfield. He passed the manse at 8:45 on the nose, month after month, returning at about 11:15. We knew he wasn't feeling well if the little black car failed to trail its quaint, friendly shadow along the pretty contours of a rural road.

Our church—like so many—failed in congregational singing. For two solid years I used all arts of diplomacy, psychology, statecraft to lure Sandy to a back pew.

"I might change my mind some day," he continued to say, holding the door open a little way. "But I'm not an easy man to convince." Nor was he.

I thought I had him when I gave him a free ticket to a men's club supper in Danielson for Monday night. But the following Sabbath provided no glimpse of the sandy expanse.

I discovered a volume he had long wished to read. I handed it to him as he sunned himself in a lounging chair in the back yard, garbed only in a pair of flashy shorts. This did not provide the sufficient impetus.

This particular day he did say something that impressed me. "If I can find a woman who reminds me of my mother, dominie, I'll take her and you'll get the long overdue pin money!"

However, how get Sandy to church? A perfectly fine voice was going to waste, the Sundays were slipping away and a pure, lyric tenor is hard to get for any church! As I mulled my severe problem, I saw his cane again hitting the cemetery turf. His mother had been interred in good Congregational earth, hadn't she? Didn't the bell, newly ringing, thanks to an agressive Dutchman, sound out over her couch of dreams? Wouldn't Sandy soon be at rest beside the one woman he adored? A thought as solemn and final as the cemetery struck solid in consciousness. I hurried down the winding Hampton Road to a picturesque dwelling, freshly painted.

Sandy was dozing in the sheltering shade of an old pear tree, his thin, bony outlines stretched at complete length in the rippling shade, birds choiring vespers overhead, tree toads and crickets adding strange music. The sun was westering. The hour was getting late.

Sandy awoke as I approached.

"Evening, dominie. Was pretty tired. Thanks for rousing me. Time for victuals."

"Sandy," I whirled upon him, "I hear your mother had a grand church funeral from the sacred altar."

He blinked those sharp eyes.

"How did you find out?"

"Never mind. I found out. And it was a large and splendid funeral."

"It sure was."

"But when your time comes you will be the only mourner at your funeral!"

"Heh, what's that?" He jumped to his feet, pulling the flashy shorts to his bony frame. "What's that you're saying?"

"Well, you don't mingle with the town people. You don't trade at the neighborhood store, or vote, or attend town hall meetings; you don't come to church. People just don't know you're alive so they won't know when you die. People will ask, 'And who was he, anyway?' Nobody will miss you. It's too bad. Your mother had such a wonderful memorial service!"

How those ocean eyes flashed about me! He swallowed hard, a half-dozen times. I can still see his Adam's apple, always obvious, moving up, down, as under power of a hidden explosion.

"Huh!" he grunted. "Now who would ever think of a thing like that?"

"I'll be there, naturally," I informed him. "But the pews will be woefully empty. If you sat in one now, many would sit in them then."

With this I excused myself, turned my preacher-black on him and vanished.

Sandy was in church next Lord's Day, and the next and the next, ad infinitum!

When he was laid to rest beside the lady he adored, the church pews were thronged and the cemetery was beautifully, radiantly alive with the many, many people who had enjoyed his exquisite tenor voice and had come to love Sandy!

Back-yard Baptism

It is not always easy to win people to the church. It is more difficult still to win an adult male. It is most difficult to win an adult male artist. And Louis Porter was no exception to the rule.

He towered over six feet in height, a gay, gallant sort, of bewitching, boyish countenance, with a topping of dark, unmanageable hair. Gracious to the point of perfection, though at the same time unconventional and sharply individualistic, we have the leading genius of the once celebrated "Connecticut Hills Art Gallery," Brooklyn, Connecticut.

Highway markers used to punctuate the state highways, their black fingers pointing tourists, guests, friends up the circuitous roads to a rural summit.

Louis and Gina purchased a valuable old house and then pondered what to do with an immense red barn across the road. Stanchions, manure, barn-sweepings were not for esthetic musings. Why not tear out a wall, put in plate glass, do some remodeling and have an art gallery for Windham County?

Calling up the road I had met the energetic, dream-seized youth and had mentioned my early artistic years, studying in Salem and Boston, painting at Beverly, Gloucester, Rockport.

Now it was Louis' turn to call on me.

"I'd like to have you as an assistant director of the gallery," he announced. "Gina and I have selected a roster of state exhibitors. We will have a slate of officers. I want you as my assistant."

"A rural pastor as an art director?" I queried.

"You will exhibit some of your marines, won't you?"

"I would like to."

"You wouldn't mind making an extra dollar, would you?"

"Not in the least."

"You will accept the nomination?"

"Why not?"

To make both ends meet during depression years in the country, I had tuned the Finnish Hall piano, worked in a Windham strawberry patch, split, stacked, piled cordwood, tended store, and run a taxi service. Here was still another turn at the wheel.

Who says that a country preacher, writing absent comrades, should excuse his brevity because his life is uneventful? One has spoken of a rural parson holding to the even tenor of his ways. Never have I found the vale of monotony.

Exhibiting paintings, greeting fellow brush-pushers, paint-daubers, clay-thumbers, studying various techniques, color schemes, drinking tea, sharing crumpets with artists and sculptors—I found certain delightful recreation.

I am looking now at an oil painting of the barn transformed into an art gallery. I have a second painting of Brooklyn-Canterbury hills, completed in an afternoon while sitting beside a cattle-bar gateway across the dirt road from the gallery. Six of us had the time of our lives that salubrious day, painting the scudding clouds and the wind-whipped trees, yelling at cows that wandered too near our easels, scooping up the bugs that nose-dived into the luscious pools of fresh paint on canvas and palette, digging easel-points into the ground when the wind became provocative.

A preacher finds good religious prospects among the artists, though he has got to do some keen word-painting and mold some compelling themes if he expects to lure these dream-children to church.

Every time I invited one sculptor to church, he retorted: "Hah, that's just a museum for dead saints! I want living experience in this world!"

Said another: "Church? It's a garage. That's where you convey your body when it's old and breaking down."

I cannot, for the life of me, remember if Louis ever listened to a sermon. I think Gina ran in for an occasional service.

Louis divulged this confession one day: "I'm not keen for ceremonials. I never hankered for preachers." He laughed, a rippling, infectious and boyish laugh; he warned me not to coax him into the musty architecture of religion. "I'm a free sort of lad," he flourished. "I was headed for the bar, but law books were too stuffy for me. Give me the winds that play about this hill, the flowers, the birds, the shadows that hide among the trees, the moons that prowl all night, the stars that dance their nightly silver minuets!"

This was Louis and, knowing him, I was stunned when he approached me one day for a religious ceremonial.

Before I tell this, an incident in the art gallery calls for acknowledgment. We had many exciting experiences in connection with our displays, appraisals, sales. One incident comes to mind this very moment. A lady of sixty, of considerable importance, exhibited her sculpture one summer. She was a most talkative, vivacious creature. She said she never suffered for an idea. Ideas were continually coming, bursting inside her like vitamins. She always had a problem child for the gallery.

One work of art that had everyone mystified was a piece of clay that it seemed had taken sick and gone into writhing labor. It was perched upon a pedestal—whatever it was—as though monarch of all it surveyed. But what was it?

"It's a bird! It's a plane! It's superman!" enthused one young sculptor as he scanned the lines.

Added another: "Can't make head or tail out of it. Am I too close? Perhaps distance will lend enchantment to the view." He moved across the floor. "I am too far now; I can't make out anything."

Inveigled a third: "Let's call it—'A Day.' You know, anything can come out of a day." The man turned to me. "Isn't there something in the Good Book along that line?"

"Boast not thyself of to morrow, for thou knowest not what a day may bring forth."

"That's it," he continued. "Who can imagine what that lump of clay in birth pangs will eventually bring forth?"

Later we begged the breezy, vivacious lady for the illuminating word. What was her masterpiece?

"Why that's an abstract idea!" she replied, a bit petulantly.

"You gentlemen are certainly familiar with the expressions and forms of modern art."

"But just what is this particular abstract idea all about?" We pressed the issue.

She withered us in a blaze of fire as she snapped: "I don't know myself! I haven't yet decided what that abstract idea will turn out to be!"

To visitors who inquired, some of us chimed with the young artist and we just called it "A Day."

Across the road from the gallery the church finally had its day. An adorable baby girl entered the childless home.

"What a work of art!" enthused the proud father. "Isn't it something! Look at the way the thing is put together! Look at the way it stuffs those fists into its mouth! Look at the way it turns up its toes!"

A living masterpiece of the Almighty, tucked under four arms, eclipsed the many scrawls of genius across the way. Here in the cradle was no feathery, vapid, abstract idea but a living, vibrant soul wrapped in beautiful colors, garnished by tenderest flesh, stars shooting from orbs of blue, music mingled with gurgled cries.

For the first time, at least to me, Louis acknowledged the supreme Artist who had most skillfully blended sculpture and painting to present a wilderness baby.

One night the father, accompanied by the mother, carried the baby into the manse. Said Louis: "We want to have the baby baptized."

My wife and I were stunned.

"You mean that, Louis?"

"I sure do. So does Gina."

"In the church?"

"No. In our back yard, among the trees, flowers, birds, the ceiling of heaven above, God's good carpet of the grass beneath, the maple trees the posts of His sanctuary, the robins and bluebirds the vested choir!"

How Louis could express himself when the mood lay on him!

Louis Porter did not come to church, but the church surely came to him one bright, cloudless Sunday afternoon. Relatives and distinguished guests came from distant places to witness the simple, happy ceremony.

What a perfectly delightful afternoon service that was! Louis held the baby girl in her exquisite baptismal white, Gina standing radiant, devout, at his side. A dear one held the baptismal bowl.

The father's eyes clung to the lively, cooing child, to her little hands dancing among the sunbeams, her bonneted head moving in rhythm with the happy fingers before the moment of baptism. His ears were tuned to this simple ritual. The mother's arm was entwined in her husband's, deeply imbedded beneath the bundle of joy.

With a bird choir in the trees, whispering winds talking to the hills, sheep bells tinkling from far, green pastures, what a time and place for an appropriate Psalm:

O come, let us sing unto the Lord: let us make a joyful noise to the rock of our salvation.

Let us come before his presence with thanksgiving, and make a joyful noise unto him with psalms.

For the Lord is a great God, and a great King above all gods;

In his hand are the deep places of the earth: the strength of the hills is his also.

The sea is his, and he made it: and his hands formed the dry land.

O come, let us worship and bow down: let us kneel before the Lord our maker;

For he is our God; and we are the people of his pasture, and the sheep of his hand. . . .

Never did the sanctuary hold more devotion, wistfulness, beauty than a summery back yard on old Tatnic Hill.

When the service was completed I noticed a strange light in the artist's eye. For once speech completely failed him. His hand, thrust into mine, spoke with an eloquence deeper than words, nobler than comment, higher than even song can go.

Let us tiptoe softly from the bed of tulips, from the grey rock garden, from the gayly cavorting sunbeams, from the lush, mellow shadows beneath the maple trees. Let us withdraw, murmuring a word from an ancient and honorable pilgrim of the vast, open spaces: "Surely the Lord is in this place."

Flame and Fury

"Honey, what's that? Wake up!"

My wife was shaking, not the daylights, but the nightfall out of me. The children were howling in the next room. I awoke with a start. Indeed, what on earth *was* going on?

From an upper window in the Brooklyn manse I stared across the dark rural road at the county jail in full illumination.

Bang! Crash! Slam-bang! Crash! Somebody was knocking the huge windows out of the jail at three o'clock in the morning.

The phone rang and I answered. "Better come over, Reverend; a man's got the d.t's. Place is a mess. Some of the boys are awful shook up." It was the warden.

Not simply the youthful inmates, but the warden, the assistant warden, the police just arriving from the Danielson barracks, the old-timers inside, indeed the buildings, the complete outfit was fearfully shaken!

An ex-prize-fighter and gambler had "gone berserk" with delirium tremens. Howling and yelling, he had smashed lavatory equipment to pieces, tearing the toilet bowl, seat, tank and sink from the wall and floor. He had used the rough pieces of crockery and metal for ammunition, heaving the toilet ruins at the heads of warden, turnkey and deputy sheriff; when they withdrew he selected windowpanes for targets.

With tear gas and drawn guns the state police finally rushed him, wrapped a strait jacket around him as in delirium he screamed: "There ain't no God, no law here, nothin'!" I watched as the police stuffed the bloody, half-dead maniac into a police car. Off to the insane asylum with this luggage!

Among the scared kids of the county jail was "Red." As I moved among the men and boys, trying to calm their fears, notifying them that order had returned from chaos, Red laid long, thin fingers on mine.

"Preacher, wasn't it wicked?"

"It's the right word, Red," I replied. "It certainly was."

"I never thought a man could go plumb loco like that."

"The end of a rotten life is just that!" I don't know why, but it seems I am always sermonizing; much of it is not intentional.

I saw Red wince up and down his lean, angular, six-foot length. He was in jail on immorality and "homo" counts. He cringed and his teeth chattered.

"Preacher, I'll never forget this night."

"Yes, remember it, Red. Vow before God that you'll never have to take such punishment."

"Could you—could you say a prayer for me?"

We stood in a jail corridor flooded with light, the incarcerated moving restlessly everywhere. I stood beside him and asked the good Lord to make Red a true, noble example of manhood.

"Thanks, preacher, thanks a lot," he said when I finished.

It is not easy to describe this bean pole of a fellow—thick, shiny red hair, long, classic face a pepper-pot of pimples, the thin, curved lips of amazing length; they were as outstanding as horizontals as his facial lines were in verticals.

When he laughed he exhibited the worst set of teeth in the county jail, nay, in the county, nay, in the country. He enjoyed laughing; but the accessories of laughing created a painful experience for every beholding lover of law and order.

When he talked he was just ordinary. But when he stood beside a battered jail upright piano to sing, Paradise opened its gates and the glory came down even into a prison-house.

After service one Sunday afternoon he inquired if I played only the hymns.

"I can play almost anything."

"Do you know 'Lilies of Lorraine,' 'Roses of Picardy,' 'Flower of Dawn,' 'Moonlight and Roses,' 'In the Garden of Tomorrow'?"

Knowing "Roses of Picardy" by heart, I struck the opening chords. I was spellbound as he closed his eyes and sang. Let me say that I have attended the Metropolitan Opera, Carnegie Hall and Town Hall presentations for twenty years but I have not listened to a tenor more purely lyrical, tenuous, bell-clear, of more exact pitch or carrying power.

"Boy, you know how to sing!" I thrilled. His voice fairly lifted me up out of the battered chair in which I sat.

"Studied two years in Providence. Mother died. Dad got running around. I mixed with the wrong crowd. I haven't sung for months until today."

"You're going to sing plenty from now on!"

I purchased the music he enjoyed. He practiced. The warden gave him the empty chapel for his exercises and soon the warden, the county commissioners and other guests, many of them men of eminence, were attending jail services to hear a voice.

One deacon, a friend of mine, drove his invalid wife one hundred miles, to park his car beneath the open window of a red-brick jail. This suffering woman received a new influx of strength and inspiration on a Sunday afternoon as Red filled her wasted soul with lilies, roses, dawn flowers and garden things.

One Sunday I talked about love to the boys.

"Love is a flower, a gorgeous rose. If you have a beautiful rose bush, how you cherish it, tend it, lift a fence around it lest the dogs trample it! You don't pick the roses, breathe their delicate fragrance once, and fling them aside. If you love —you cherish—a girl—the same way." I went on.

Red asked me to repeat "the rose-bush sermon" the following Sunday. He asked for a typescript of it.

A month later he was again impressed. A devout Roman priest had left a tiny, shiny crucifix in the chapel. I held it aloft before fifty men and boys sitting on rough, hard benches.

"Boys!" I announced. "Within the shadow of the cross we are all brothers, or, to use the Master's word—friends."

In that quiet, thoughtful hour I was led to open my heart to this sad, wistful congregation. I recall saying words like these:

"Boys, I believe in you. You have God and youth and the good life calling to you. You can climb the hill and make every grade. Why not?"

A brief, pungent quatrain from the great traveler, Robert W. Service, came to mind. I voiced it.

Yes, if you're a tramp in tatters,
While the blue sky bends above
You've got nearly all that matters—
You've got God, and God is love.[1]

While words of simple rhyme vibrated in the stiflingly hot and cramped room, barred windows obstructing the view of the open road, faces brightened, forms relaxed, eyes softened.

It seemed that a vision of a rose bush twining about a cross beneath a God-arched sky was beginning to intrigue the spare, listless tenor. A new tremulo was sounding off somewhere in the invisible organ when he sang. Even hard-boiled men turned faces to bare walls when he wove mother's portrait in a web of wondrous song and placed it before them.

And then, one clear, sunlit morning he knocked at the side door of the manse. I opened it. Red was elegantly clothed; recognizing him, I blinked in astonishment.

For a full minute he struggled for words, then he stammered: "My time is done. The record's clean. But—but—I'm too scared to go home."

"What is it, Red?"

He held a brief case stuffed with sheet music. A dear lady, a county commissioner, had presented him with it for good behavior.

"I asked the cops to run me home; they wouldn't; said it was beyond their jurisdiction."

"How far away is your home?"

He told me. It was in a small, dairy community some fifteen miles away.

[1] Robert W. Service, "Comfort," from *The Spell of the Yukon*. Reprinted by permission of Dodd, Mead & Company.

"Father has a housekeeper. She hates me. I'll say things I shouldn't when we meet. I thought that if the police had a little talk with her, it might ease things a little, kind of soften up home-coming."

"I'll be glad to run you home."

"You will? Gee, that's great!"

"We are just sitting down to coffee, fried eggs, pancakes and maple syrup. Will you join us?"

"I didn't eat breakfast; felt pretty jumpy," he divulged. The long, thin head glowed in the radiant sun of early morning.

"Come on in, Red; have your cup of coffee with me."

I took his coat. My wife slipped another chair up to the kitchen table where four children encircled him, tall, dawn-lovely Priscilla, Wendell, Bruce and Rupert. My wife handed him a steaming plate.

Red stared at the six of us, pulled himself from the table, looked out a manse window across the road at a ponderous red-brick outline, paced the humble floor a few moments crying like a baby, wiping tears on a raised coatsleeve. My wife gave him a handkerchief.

It was just a summer shower. He returned to the table, his face reflecting a challenge.

"To think that I'm fit, fit to sit at this table with you folks!" He dared not venture another word.

"Why aren't you good enough?" challenged Wendell, the pretty, talkative lad of five years.

I quoted the four lines he had come to enjoy.

Yes, if you're a tramp in tatters,
While the blue sky bends above
You've got nearly all that matters—
You've got God, and God is love.

Soon I was having a private session, not with the kindly mistress of the manse, that very morning the angel of the kitchen, but with a stoop-shouldered, heavily-built, surly woman. Red lingered in his father's yard until I emerged from the secret conference.

"Take my music in for me," he said. "I'd like to have you go with me to my room."

He was always the perfect gentleman in my presence.

"Be sure to read the Bible and to pray," I advised him when leaving. "Remember the rose bush, the cross and the blue sky."

"I will, preacher. Honest I will."

I heard that my friend left his unhappy father's house and went to a distant city to find work.

Only once did I lay eyes on him again. He was walking the sunlit pavements of Danielson, a large, wholesome-looking woman at his side. She was blue-eyed, wore an enormous hat, walked with fine, noble gait and the hair wrapped in a huge pug below the bonnet's rim was a shining red! He grabbed hold of me.

"Preacher, meet the better half! We got spliced last year. I got a swell job. Flora is a wonderful cook and she can play the piano!"

"Do you still sing?"

"You betcha! Flora says I'm going to be learning lullabyes and cradle songs one of these days!"

Did he laugh!

And did I behold a most immaculate set of perfect teeth!

I returned to my rural manse that day and the roads were seams of magic carpets, the trees were a wonderful whispering gallery and every breeze and sunbeam were singing, in fact the whole landscape was singing neatly and in tune Robert Browning's happy words:

The year's at the spring
And day's at the morn;
Morning's at seven;
The hill-side's dew-pearled;
The lark's on the wing;
The snail's on the thorn;
God's in his heaven—
All's right with the world!

Fortunes of a Week

Two girls and a boy broke into the presumably quiet career of a country preacher one never-to-be-forgotten week. Sometimes I think we would do well to confine in jail the person who wrote the familiar song: "It's so peaceful in the country."

Charlotte Cummings, sixteen, was the first to startle me, calling me from the supper table. She was telephoning from Willimantic.

"Oh, pastor, father has been arrested. He was driving the car under his old license. And he passed another bad check."

"Where is your father?"

"He's in the police station."

"Well, what am I supposed to do?"

"Come down and get him out."

"How can I do that if he's in the custody of the police?"

"The captain says he will let father out overnight if you will take the responsibility. Father has to be in court in the morning. He can come home if you will come and take him home and promise to have him back for court at nine-thirty."

For many years Charlotte's father had been a problem to the state, the church, the police. I had been paying for his electric lights for months. The Connecticut Light & Power Co. had refused to let him have service under his own signature. He would promise one thing and practice another. He was the despair of social workers, county detectives, lawyers.

The sad fact was that seven children looked upon him as an example of fatherhood. Five of them came to Sabbath school if I drove three miles after them. Charlotte was the oldest, a splendid, well-meaning girl. She was most urgent as she talked to me.

"I told the captain I would call you. I told him I knew you would accept the responsibility for father."

It was risky to go bail for Jake Cummings, or to make any definite statement to the authorities, but who could hurt the faith of an eager teen-ager who loved her father, regardless of his history?

"I will be right down, Charlotte."

Naturally I was nervous when I pledged the police that I would have him back in the morning. I did not rest well all night. What a relief when I found Jake dressed, ready for the ride to court in the morning! His wife and the seven children piled into the car. The court had mercy on the family and, feeling for the bedraggled mother and children, placed Jake on probation again.

He entered a nearby church when released, hurried to the altar-rail and knelt in prayer, thanking God for deliverance.

Returning home he aroused the indignation of the state with his irregular performances within two months.

The first crisis had hardly passed when a second girl's voice came pouring in over the phone. Yvonne was eighteen years of age, worked in a thread mill, a pasty, sickly looking girl.

"Reverend, is that you? Come down at once. Judy is dying. She got shot! Hurry!"

Traveling seventy miles an hour I dashed along a winding stretch of rural road to a flat, ramshackle farmhouse in the deep thickets. Police cars had preceded me to the grim appointment.

"Judy's dead already," a sister of sixteen cried hysterically as I started toward the house.

"Oh, Reverend!" screamed the fourteen-year-old sister. "The baby is dead! Dead this very minute!"

The mother was frantic, wailing at the top of her voice: "It can't be! Not my baby dead! Not my little darling dead!"

The father, a woodsman, large and robust, led me to a form under a blanket on a bed.

"Say a prayer, minister. She's gone. But say a prayer just the same. We thought we could save her; we couldn't."

What was the reason for this tragedy? The reason was a twelve-year-old boy who had fled into the woods. The brother had, against orders, gone into his father's gun closet. The father was a celebrated hunter, a crack shot. The lad had discovered a shiny revolver in the collection. His little sister had followed him upstairs. Demonstrating the revolver, he had made a target of the stomach of his playful sister. The trigger was touched; a bullet tore into the body of the child, who fell screaming to the floor.

"But, ma, I didn't know it was loaded!" the brother shrieked as, panic-stricken, he saw his sister lying in a pool of blood and then streaked into the woods.

Later that day the lieutenant of the state police said to me: "Keep your eye on that boy. He is likely to become a mental case over this. Naturally the entire family looks on him now as an outcast. The next week will be a critical one for him!"

The funeral was inexpressibly tragic.

I saw a strong man, woodsman of years, proud hunter, go to pieces. The mother never recovered from the blow. We had a fierce battle on our hands to save twelve-year-old Harry from the woods, from his family, from himself.

Charlotte called Monday evening; Yvonne called Wednesday morning and on Friday night little Tommy Jenkins called. (This time it was a boy.) A frightened, tremulous voice came to me out of the night.

"There's thieves here, Reverend. They're trying to break in the house. Mother thinks they're drunk. They're making an awful racket outside the house. We're here alone, mother and us. Dad is away. Can you come down?"

What pastor relishes a trip in the dark night to a forsaken farm under such conditions? The farmhouse was a summer home for city people, of another religious sect. The three boys often attended our church school in the summertime.

"Mother's awful scarey, Reverend. We're all scarey. Can't you come down?"

"Sure. I will be down as soon as I can get there."

Was I a trifle nervous as I turned my car down a pitch-black rural road? Did my imagination conjure up some harsh, menacing images? Did I ask myself how to grapple with two thugs—or more—in the wilderness? Did I direct headlights in all latitudes and longitudes as I slipped from the four corners down a sharp glade along a scimitar-road to a lonely, embattled dwelling? I did.

Moving cautiously, praying, hoping against hope, I approached the solitary farmhouse, lights in the upper windows, the lower floor blacked out. Honking the horn to let the vandals know that salvation had arrived, slamming the car door to enhance the conviction, I stepped into the yard in the blaze of the headlamps.

"What's going on here?" I cried in loud, parsonic tones, boasting strength. "Who's disturbing the peace?"

Is it easy to snoop around in the dark expecting villains to rush from behind posts, sheds, trees, to fire into one's back from behind a ghostly wall or ghastly fence? Yes, I endeavored to put up a brave front, but I was shaking in my shoes every step of the way!

"Who's disturbing the peace around here?" I trumpeted again.

There was no answer, no rustling in the summer grass, no movement beneath the stacked trees. I turned eyes and ears upon a huge barn across the dirt road, its black outline lifted against a black sky. All seemed quiet over there.

I crept toward the rear of the house—the headlamps flooding the back yard—to examine a woodshed. The culprits must be hiding somewhere. I listened to hear a motor wake the echoes of the stilly night. There must be a parked car around somewhere. Night held her tongue; there was no kind of interruption save an upper window opening cautiously.

"Is that you, pastor?"

A woman's shaky voice disturbed the dense silence.

"Yes, it's I."

"We've had a perfectly dreadful time the last hour! Somebody has been prowling around, banging around the place. I am sure there was more than one. We've been just about scared out of our wits!"

"All is quiet now."

"Yes, for the moment. They'll probably be back as soon as you go. And my husband couldn't come out until tomorrow. Isn't that always the way? Here I am with the three boys and a little girl in this great house without protection."

"I'll be glad to stay a while until the thing clears up," I promised.

"You will? Oh, thank you so much! Tommy will go down and unlock the door and let you in."

Tea was served, sandwiches, crackers—a late snack.

At one o'clock I decided I might return to the manse. All was under control along the Canterbury ridge.

Imagine my surprise an hour later when my wife and I and our four children were roused from sleep by a pounding and banging near our house; steps rushed everywhere. Heavy bodies seemed about to tramp down the front door. There was heaving, a pounding, a panting in the back yard.

"Those rascals have come for us now," chattered my wife. And then the racket ceased as suddenly, as unaccountably, as it had started.

In the morning, going into the garden, I found my garden a mess and in the soft loam I noticed the split hoof-prints of two huge stags. I hurried to Tommy and his folks. Sure enough! In their back yard we spied the same tell-tale hoof-prints and in a large garden were the same depredations.

"Those were the rascals!" was a parson's Saturday morning word of knowledge, pointing to the ground.

Was I in the proper mood to preach on the serenity and comfort of our faith on the Lord's Day?

Even today an invitation to "a stag party" sends the cold chills over me.

Was it a week!

Now, where is that lyrical youngster who had the sublime audacity to prattle, "It's so peaceful in the country"?

Hospital Tragedy

"Is the Reverend there? Please, Mrs. Cleveland, try to reach him. Have him call me at home. It is terribly urgent."

"I think he is studying at the Norwich Library."

"Will you try to get him?"

"I'll do my best."

What a transition, from an absorbing volume of ancient history into the boiling vortex of the living present! One of the librarians asked me to call my home. My wife gave me Harold Peterson's phone number.

"What is it, Harold?"

"Margaret's dead."

"What? Not your wife?"

"Yes, and the kids are in school and they don't know it. I—I'm lost, Reverend. I don't know what to do. Please come over—at once!"

I had met Harold a year earlier on a beautiful Connecticut hill. He had purchased a splendid farm. His children must grow up in the beauty and dignity of the country.

When I arrrived at the house I faced a broken, staggered man. It seemed he had aged fifty years in the five days since I had talked with him. He narrated a tragic story.

Margaret, his wife, was troubled with sinus. A specialist in a large city had met her as he examined the youngest boy's tonsils. He promised to relieve the mother by a minor operation. He could straighten her out in twenty minutes. There wasn't anything at all to the operation.

The night before Margaret had checked into the hospital. Harold, who had continued working at an aircraft factory while building up a neglected farm, went to work in the morning as usual, expecting to find his wife home for supper. A half hour after reporting for work he received a phone call from the hospital: "Your wife . . . is . . . dead."

Hurried, this particular morning, the nurse in charge had failed to test Mrs. Peterson for the local anesthetic administered. Within five minutes the pretty, vivacious Swedish mother lay on the operating table—a corpse.

A rural pastor soon finds that he must try to do his solemn work in a world of sudden, climactic tragedy. Harold's voice faltered as he talked, his pure Swedish tenor lost its lyrical quality. His sea-chrome eyes went wild.

"I could kill that doctor!" he exploded. "Margaret, my wonderful Margaret, dead! That doctor talked her into that hospital trip; he didn't check on the nurse, or the anesthetic. He's no better than a murderer. I'll kill him! I'll sue him for every last cent he has!"

One cannot describe such intense and fearful agony. Harold didn't weep; it seemed he was pouring out his soul in agony.

"Reverend, my children are in school—Jenny and Carl and little Arthur. They don't know anything's wrong. How shall I break the news? What can I say to them when they come home and there's no Mommie to welcome them—and won't be any more?"

Pastors face hours of grim terror and fierce, crucial need. This hour was one of the blackest that ever dragged me in under the blackness. I really don't remember what I said about breaking the news to the youngsters. Harold was doing most of the talking, making threats, pledging cruel reprisals, vindictive as I have never known a human being to be.

"Reverend, what can we do?" he finally sobbed.

"We can pray. Frankly, I don't know what else we can do. We need wisdom, guidance, help. We must be so careful as we deal with the children, specially little Arthur."

"It will be cruel, wicked for Artie!" cried Harold, his words a wail rather than words.

"In the beginning, God. . . ." The words opening the long pages of Holy Writ came to me.

"Harold," I suggested, "we've got to begin this long, hard work of reconstruction with God's help. Men have made this chaos; only God can bring order into the chaos now, even as in the beginning."

"Perhaps you're right, Reverend. I can't pray. If you can, go ahead."

Even prayer did not come easily—the thoughts, the words, the voice to express thoughts in words.

Neighbors, hearing the grim news, visited the house. A farm housewife nearby washed and dried the breakfast dishes, swept the kitchen. She would prepare supper. Friends began to arrive.

Is it a simple thing for a pastor to accompany a stricken man to select a casket? Harold nearly fainted dead away in the undertaker's rooms.

"I'll never go . . . through . . . this," he panted, his voice failing.

"You've got to, for the sake of the children," I insisted. "Harold, you've just got to bear up."

For a few minutes his mind became a total blank under the crushing burden of sorrow. He couldn't recall the names of her brothers or sisters. After resting a few moments his mind cleared.

It was difficult to inform thirteen-year-old Jenny that she was now motherless, to break the news to Carl, who was ten years old. The heartbreaking moment was when little Arthur, rushing into the yard from a noisy school bus, seeing the strangers, exclaimed: "Where's my Mommie?"

Harold threw his arms about the lad, led him across the yard to the barn and there, alone, struggling with a failing voice, moment to moment, choked out the cruel narrative.

A pastor must spend considerable time with a man in this crisis, not for an hour or a week end, but for many weeks. Harold's hatred toward a careless physician, a neglectful nurse, did not abate easily or early. Even today, ten years later, it is not wise to mention the subject.

"I don't know whether there is a God or not! I don't know if it pays to try to be good! I don't know if a man gets a thing out of church!" Often pain filled Jenny's eyes when her father talked like that and little Arthur stared so strangely at him.

"Harold," I challenged often, "do you want your children to grow up atheists, imbeciles, fools, scorning the moral law? Because a doctor failed to do his duty one day, does that knock

God off His throne? Honestly, sometimes you talk like a heathen. Little ears, little hearts are taking this in!"

"I suppose you're right. I suppose I ought to be more careful. But if you could only know, Reverend, what's going on inside me, you might wonder that I don't say more. Night after night I've had to fight—to fight the drive to go to a certain doctor's home and wind things up!"

"Yes, and then your beautiful children, *her* lovely children, would be cast adrift upon the world without a father. Isn't it enough that they have been denied a mother? Would you, by your own act, deny them the love and care of a father? That would indeed be double trouble."

I think I pierced his vulnerable spot the night I voiced that homely bit of philosophy in the hen coop as he gathered eggs. His tirades against time, tide, circumstances did not seem quite so vicious in the oncoming days.

There was one other night during a late lunch when he lost hold of himself. "Reverend!" he exclaimed hysterically. "Why should I live? There's nothing now for me to live for!"

"Nothing?" I howled back at him, staring at three motherless children sitting at the table.

With a suffocating cry, Jenny lurched to her feet and rushed from the kitchen; we heard her footfalls dying away on the floor overhead.

"I'm a fool!" he expostulated, bolting the table and following his girl upstairs.

Night after night he poured out his soul, confessed his fears and doubts and hatreds. Nevertheless, little by little the terribly bitter flood tide commenced to ebb; the invectives had a tendency to soften, the curses were less vicious, the angry outbursts not so volcanic.

"Things must straighten out better than this."

What else could one say?

The children were wonderful. Each child crept closer to the father in the sad, lonely hours of bereavement. Jenny was truly marvelous. She became a little mother to the boys; we all stood amazed as she made faith, courage, fortitude visible in the home. "I shall grow up," she promised, "exactly the way Mother wanted me to grow up." She decided to become a nurse; she would make sure that tragic oversights didn't happen.

Night after night Harold found the bitter moods softening, the hateful threats breaking up in the hour of prayer. Music assuaged the heartache a little. When we read the Good Book he seemed to relax.

"Pray, Reverend, pray," he would say, night after night, for weeks, months, as Jenny brought out late snacks to the kitchen table. Harold would eat fairly well during these late fellowship hours. Following coffee, sandwiches, doughnuts, Swedish pastries, we would bend heads around Margaret's table, think about her, recall her sweet, girlish expression, the thick blonde hair, the nicely contoured, childlike lips and bless and honor her in prayer. And these were Harold's most comfortable moments and things did begin to straighten out better.

A noble, efficient lady met Harold, a lady who had not married, a lady who loved children. Jenny and Carl moved into her arms as metal to its magnet. Artie climbed up into her heart and soon another mother was tucking him in bed.

Today the Swedish tenor sings again; the splendid home is no longer a haunt of shadows. The nights are literally filled with music.

Reopening a closed church in his neighborhood, I had first driven to the green-clad summit where we met. So wonderful is life! Today my own baby boy, Bruce, is pastor of that reopened church. And Harold, his wife, and the three children comprise one of the most radiant and steadfast church families in that beautiful area.

In fact I have a hunch that things have straightened out for everyone much more pleasantly than any of us could possibly have imagined!

Role of a Redhead

"Prea—preach—er, my woman, she is not right. She wants to—to see—you."

I knew the voice, that of Bunko Rockwell, the Wyoming cowboy. He drawled; he stammered; it was sometimes painful to try to carry on a conversation with him. He had told me the derivation of his nickname. He liked to sleep under trees on the range.

"I reckon I'd *bunk* anywhere efn it was a tree," he drawled. Bunko Rockwell—he was thus "nighted" and described by the cowhands. His nickname followed him across the trails into eastern Connecticut.

A neighbor brought the oldest boy and the girl to the Sunday school. I had called at their small grey-green cottage a score of times.

Bunko, who met me as I drove into the yard, was fifty

years of age, small of build, with a glass eye, a fearfully pale face, a lisping, stammering tongue. He had one flourishing element: that crop of jet black hair! It leaped up, poured out of his scalp; one would think it a woman's bobbed hair, so thick and luxuriant it was! I forbear to describe the lisping, stammering speech further.

"Eloise is acting strange. She can't eat or sleep. She is awful jittery, preacher. She is in the house. Go on in."

One never entered the tiny cottage built for two people, now housing six, soon to shelter eight, without becoming aware of wet diapers, without seeing boys in dirty shirts and wet pants crawling all over the place. Eloise sat in a rather delapidated parlor chair holding a squalling baby, another of sixteen months pulling at the chair's velours.

"Morning, preacher."

She greeted me with a gentle, singing voice. When she spoke I recalled the lines from Elizabeth Barrett Browning's "A Musical Instrument":

> Sweet, sweet, sweet, O Pan!
>   Piercing sweet by the river!
> Blinding sweet, O great god Pan!
> The sun on the hill forgot to die,
> And the lilies revived, and the dragonfly
> Came back to dream on the river.

Eloise was as attractive, appealing, old-fashioned as her name; twenty-three years old, of oval, exquisite face, slender of form, gracious in manner and language. Her bright red, silken hair was tied and looped in two braids, head to shoulder. How was it that so stunning a girl had married blunt, awkward, stuttering Bunko?

When I inquired the reason for her apparent nervousness, she led me outdoors into the tiny yard.

"Velma and Billy were playing here yesterday when a copperhead came out of the woods." She shuddered. "The snake wiggled almost to Velma's feet. She screamed. Billy aimed a rock at the varmint and it went back under the trees." She was trembling; her breast heaved with emotion.

"I don't believe there are any copperheads around here," I told her.

"From what Billy said I reckon it was a copperhead," Bunko judged.

For the next few months Eloise increased in nervousness. Billy, seven years old, was not getting along well in the village school.

Bunko had moved to Connecticut because relatives had preceded him east. He worked hard in a lumber mill. The two infant sons were ill most of the time. People seemed to be calling Eloise on the phone and laughing because a pretty girl married an old Western codger. We never did get to the bottom of this mystery.

I called on her one day, Billy having admitted in Sunday school that his mother was "plumb tuckered out," and Eloise made a confession. With what pain and shame she slowly divulged the secret, why she had married Bunko and moved east!

"We lived on a ranch. Mother died. Dad was a hard worker. A second woman—not much good—brought me up. She let me go out with anybody. She never told me to be careful.

"After a late dance it happened, one night. My companion, a boy of seventeen—I was just turning sixteen—said he loved me. What did I know about love? Dad was too busy on the range to love me. The woman who brought me up worked me like a horse. I wondered what love was. I was just a kid, didn't know anything.

"I was sorry, the next day. In fact, I cried all night. I knew I hadn't done right. That wasn't love. But the baby came. I cried and prayed, but the baby came. I had Billy before I was seventeen. The father skipped away to a city.

"Oh, preacher, if you only knew what I went through then —when Billy was born, the way people talked! I was even insulted in church. No good man would come near me. Cheap, mean men who wouldn't settle down, men who beat their wives and drank, they all came hanging around. I was almost crazy when Bunko showed up. He hadn't married. Said he'd take the kid if he had to, to get me. He'd move away; he'd give me a home. He'd come east; he's got a sister in Norwich.

"Now that sister's got talking and somebody told Velma, five years old, our first child, that Billy isn't her real brother. I don't know what to do. Yon know, Billy's my boy and I love him. I've suffered so much, getting him, keeping him, that I can't bear to hear these things.

"Preacher, do you think God holds it against me because I think so much of Billy, because I fight for him? Am I really, truly a sinful woman?"

The wretched sorrows of a whole world, it seems, are at times heaped at the rural pastor's feet. Who would not feel pity, sympathy for a twenty-three-year-old redhead who had traveled a hateful road? She was becoming old and careworn at twenty-three.

The unhappy story did get out and Eloise mourned. A neighbor, a churchwoman, finding that this marriage seemed one of convenience, finding Eloise worn out having babies, advised her to divorce Bunko. I rushed to one prim, decorous home and suggested that a religious woman read her Bible and mind her own business. She might start with "Blessed are the merciful, for they shall obtain mercy"; "Judge not, that ye be not judged"; "What God hath joined together let not man—nor woman—put asunder."

Before the fifth child came, Eloise began to fear the future's shadows. Everything bothered her. She was surrounded by a culture that criticizes suffering people instead of challenging them.

Facing her one day in the small, damp living room, full of broken toys and squalling babies, I said: "I think Bunko should give you more attention."

"He works hard in the mill, preacher. He comes home and drops in the chair; in five minutes he's asleep. He isn't feeling good lately."

"But he might take you for a ride in the country; he might drive you to the shore; he could run you up to church and baby-sit on a Sunday morning. I think he might express a little more love to you."

Eloise began to tremble; fear covered her like a blanket. "No, not love, preacher. I don't want him to love me any more; he loves me too much now. I'm going to have another baby. Every year I have one—and I'm getting so weak, bringing boys into the world!"

Suddenly I sensed that I had a real challenge on my hands, to unfold the Christian meaning of love to this gentle and frightened girl.

One Friday morning Bunko called again. Eloise was really bad. Her mind was unbalanced. A neighbor had come to the cottage, trying to comfort her. I called in the afternoon and again in the evening as I was driving home a mother and her eight children from the weekly prayer service. A district nurse had hurried away only a minute earlier. A doctor had just arrived.

"She needs a good long rest," diagnosed the physician. "She

needs a psychiatric retreat. If that cannot be managed financially, she must enter a state institution."

"I'll take home the folks I have in the car and be back in ten minutes. If we must, we will take her to Norwich," I told Bunko and the doctor.

Eloise had said at first that she would not leave the family. Finally she admitted she would go to Norwich with her husband and the preacher, if they thought it best.

Ten minutes later I hurried back to the tiny cottage.

"Where's Eloise?"

Stammered Bunko: "The police came and got her."

"What?"

"Yes. The neighbor who was here called a sheriff; he sent the police. They came with cops and guns and got her. Eloise was plumb scared out of her wits!"

Indeed, she was most literally scared out of her wits! I had missed the state police by split seconds. The redhead never forgave Bunko for not holding up the police car for another five minutes.

Weak and exhausted as she was, the sight of uniforms, particularly guns, terrified her, drove in upon her already too sensitive consciousness the fact that she was a bad woman. If not, why did the *police* come for her? In Wyoming the police had come to see her. And now the stern authorities had moved in again.

When I called on the young mother at the state hospital she was starting the shock treatments. She had lucid moments and many confused hours.

"Preacher, I wish I could have my pocketbook with my false teeth, my mirror and comb."

No person is so lost and bereaved in this world as a woman who has lost her pocketbook.

"Preacher, I wish I could sleep better. I have no appetite. I hope Billy is doing all right in school and people are nice to him."

When I said her husband would be down on Saturday her face darkened, a hoarseness crept into the singing voice as though sandpaper moved across the finish: "He let those men with guns push me into the car and take my baby away from me. If he loved me, why did he let them push me around?"

In a few months Eloise could stand behind wire-netted windows and gaze upon her children in an institutional yard; from an upper, barred window she could smile and wave to them and throw them goodbye kisses.

She returned home to a family of seven and not six. In another five months she had definitely improved.

Then Bunko called the manse again: "Preacher, I think you ought to come down."

Eloise was once more pacing about the narrow, wet rooms amid broken toys, squalling babies, dirty walls, sagging chairs. Her handsome red hair was dishevelled; her cheeks were bloated and there was a tragic film over the once gay, laughing eyes of Wyoming blue.

"I'm not happy," she confessed in mournful tones. "People don't want me here. Billy is persecuted in school. Bunko won't take me any place."

"I really think he loves you—in his way," I assuaged.

"Yes, perhaps in his way," she admitted, a rising, stern note in her throat, her once handsome girlish face in a grimace. "I'm to have another baby, no doubt a boy, and I haven't—haven't the strength to have him. Do you call that love, preacher, to fill the home with boys till I can't tend to them? Should I have so many? And will I get so sick I got to go back to that awful place? No! I won't go back! I'll die before I go back!"

Eloise changed in a moment of time. She became loud, incriminating, cruel. "I can't stand that racket again, women howling all night, banging the place to pieces, laughing like devils laugh, telling their dirty stories, poking me in the ribs, pulling the leaves out of my Bible! They talk to the birds, the winds, the trees, grin like pumpkins, tear off every stitch of clothes and—O God!"

Yes, I knew what would happen. The doctor said she would go into a temporary unbalanced condition for the first few months of pregnancy. There was a second trip to the state institution. This time slimmer, more solemn, Eloise returned to the cramped, noisy rooms that imposed a burden of six children on her slowly diminishing strength.

Bunko carried her to church just once.

"I think the church is what I need," she confessed one day. "I'm a sinner and the Lord was the friend of poor sinners. I believe He would forgive me if I could get to Him. I don't know as I've tried as hard as I should to get to Him."

We had prayer together and the following Sabbath Eloise sat in an ancient Pilgrim pew, Velma on her left, Billy on her right. Where did I find a good text? Look at Jeremiah 30:17:

> For I will restore health unto thee, and I will heal thee of thy wounds, saith the Lord; because they called thee an Outcast, saying, This is Zion, whom no man seeketh after.

Within a month the redhead received a letter from Wyoming. Nobody knows how Billy's father ever procured the Connecticut address. But he did get hold of it and Eloise received a letter. She cried, stormed, burned the letter; but it had burned terribly deep into her subconsciousness.

Bunko had been complaining about an upset stomach, pains

in his side and back for a year. He finally went to see the doctor.

"You are full of cancer; you can't live six months." The physician gave his ultimatum.

"I'm going to make my last bunk under the Wyoming trees," Bunko declared.

Soon there was a little cottage for sale and Bunko, Eloise and six youngsters piled into an old black car that turned about and, like the Wyoming herds, went home. Eloise wrote a neighbor five months later that her husband was sleeping beneath the good, green grass of Wyoming.

Has she discovered the beauty, the wonder, the ecstasy of the more abundant life? Have Wyoming skies told her a thing? I wonder. I have a hunch I shall always wonder.

The Incredible Battle

A newspaper columnist, a devout Roman Catholic, stopped at the door one morning.

"I've just visited a man in Eastford. I think you ought to see him. He served as a New Deal director under Roosevelt. He's in terrible shape in a dingy room with multiple sclerosis, going blind. That guy, Reverend, really needs a pep talk. I wouldn't wait around too long before looking him up."

Chauncey Francis Gunnerson was, indeed, what F. D. R. labelled "the forgotten man." In an upper room I met him, sitting on an unmade bed, cane at his side, crutches against the wall; dingy curtains were half drawn, a tiny stove and empty tin cans in one dark corner of the room, old, mangy clothes tossed into another; dust-laden books, magazines, papers were stacked in another; pills, bottles, medicines littered a cheap table in still another.

Mingled odors of dust, empty cans, medicines almost overwhelmed me as I entered the single, dirty room which had become a celebrated politician's complete empire!

"Who are you?" a halting voice inquired, as the good eye moved my way, the nearly blind one hidden behind a leather patch. A stout, thickset man tried to pull himself up from the unmade bed at 3 P.M., only to stagger dizzily and drop back. He panted in the throes of exertion, extending the left hand for greeting. The right hand was fearfully swollen and of unnatural high color.

I told Chauncey about the visit from a newsman and that I was making a friendly call.

"Yes, Dave told me he would see you. You know, Reverend, I'm in a bad way, going blind, fighting multiple sclerosis. Look at me! I'm a sight!"

His words were beautifully spoken, perfectly articulated. There was a certain dignity even in his misery. The unshaven face suggested classic lines; the iron-grey hair was even mussed with distinction; there was a note of authority in the nervous toss of his large head.

"Joe Eastman was my best friend," he enthused as he turned to one dingy wall and pointed out a large photograph. "I used to sit in conferences with the big boys, had my own office. I kept half of this area in sugar, beef, lumber, coffee. But for me, dozens of local businessmen would have gone on the rocks. I went to bat for New England again and again. And now New England has left me to rot in this hole!"

He struggled some with words; he labored to breathe, he grabbed his right side, moaned, winced with pain, waited a full minute before continuing his narrative.

"I'm breaking up," he confessed. "On the way out. Never thought the end could be like this. Think of me, spreading my table with porterhouse steaks for the civil, social leaders of New England, now scooping cold bean soup out of a can! Look at my kitchen now!" He pointed to a black, tiny electric stove in a corner, cans, empty, not empty, flanking it like a stockade.

"What is a man of your eminence and quality, having served his nation as Dave says you served it, doing in a place like this?" I questioned.

"I got sick. I all but died in another town. On what was supposed to be my dying bed, I gave my property to some friends. They took my things—all of them—and I somehow failed to die. Now I cannot lay hands on my own property, my record library, my electronic equipment, even my false teeth!"

"What? Get a lawyer!"

"No lawyer will touch my case. Big names are involved in what might become a public scandal."

"You have appealed to the state?"

"The state supplies my bare necessities. It will do no more."

"You have appealed to the press?"

"The big, powerful dailies will not print my story."

"You have no relatives?"

"No wife, no child, nobody. A kind woman let me have this room."

"You have a car?"

"It's in the yard; it's been sitting there on its haunches two solid years, just crumbling away like its owner."

"Is this the best New England can do for you?" I believe I spoke sharply, violently for a minister.

"Wait—wait," he said, struggling to his feet, grasping the the cane beside the bed, trying to get his unruly legs to behave, his body testing various degrees of vertical position to arise, to work out a walking posture. Impossible! He fell back again upon his bed.

"It's no use, no use, Reverend." He proceeded to quote a quatrain from club-footed Lord Byron.

> My days are in the yellow leaf,
> The flowers and fruits of love are gone;
> The worm, the canker and the grief
> Are mine alone.

He used me for his errand boy around the confines of the dark room. He showed me letters, orders, congratulations, materials proving his position of high responsibility.

"Yes, I was somebody once," he declared. "Now that I'm sick, of no use to anybody, they let me rot here. Once the businessmen of this area haunted my office for favors. I did pull wires for New England. And what has New England done for me? It has given me an incurable illness, weakened my heart, taken my house, grabbed my money, shoved me into an attic!"

There is no doubt Chauncey was embittered and vindictive. He was amazingly independent and his words of incrimination hard and violent. Perhaps there were reasons why many people feared to lift up his fallen, shell-shot flag.

I turned upon him.

"You will stay here in this suffocating place and rot, no doubt about it, unless you get hold of three facts—and get hold right away!"

My sudden transition into the pastoral role seemed to rouse him to other matters.

"What do you mean?"

"This vitriolic acid of yours can eat your mind and soul away. You've got to start fighting."

"You think, Reverend, I haven't fought?" He leered at me; his haughty, ironic eye, the good one, was fierce enough to singe.

"Yes, with carnal weapons, but not with spiritual."

"Sermons! Sermons!" he exclaimed with disdain. "When you ministers come up against a tough proposition you start bandying sermons about. You never face reality."

Ignoring his criticism I continued: "You need God; you need the Bible; you need the will to believe!"

My hot shot hit home.

"You . . . you have just quoted William James," he stammered. "What do you know about him?"

"One thing I know. I know that you don't know him, you with your explosive pessimist conclusions. What did James say?"

"Well, what did he say?"

"What is concluded that we may conclude about it?"

"He said that."

"Yes, and more, a great deal more."

"I always enjoyed the lively psychology of William James and the philosophy of Josiah Royce, both Harvard men."

"Yes, Gunnerson, I have in my library most of the books of Josiah Royce."

"Well! Well!" For the moment only this word interested him.

"But to get back to my theme, Gunnerson. If you could grasp the dynamic concept of God; if you could really grasp the teachings of the Holy Bible, especially the thrilling words of Christ; if you could enter into activity with the will to believe, you could get back on your feet, you could drive that car in the yard, you could commence the physical, spiritual rehabilitation of life!"

"You . . . really . . . think . . . it . . . possible?"

"I do. Not at once. Not in the dark, dingy negative of your yesterdays. But if you can grasp the thought of God over this sickroom, a Nazarene living in and guiding the world, grab hold of His words—'Arise, take up thy bed and walk!' —who knows? Do you pray?"

He grinned, I must say, a silly, foolish grin.

"What could prayer do for me?"

"Have you tried?" I pinned him down for answer.

"No."

"You have no use for William James. You are no pragmatist. You don't know if prayer works; you never gave it half a try. Do you read the New Testament? Have you got one?"

"I don't know. I was too busy for church."

"I'm not talking church. I'm asking you if you have gathered into your shrunken, starved soul the great, powerful substance, the food in the timeless teachings of Christ."

"But what good—"

Brushing his objection to one side I finished: "And could you rouse in yourself the will to believe in the reality of God, the power of Christ, you might surprise yourself to note what could happen."

"You think . . . I could . . . drive my car again and move about the world . . . on my own, not in an ambulance?"

"Is there any harm in trying?"

"I don't know," he said slowly.

"O God," I prayed, holding the red, swollen hand as I prepared to leave. "O God, have mercy on this sad, suffering man. Let him lay hold of the three facts. Rouse his mind, stir up his dormant spirit. Plunge his naked soul into the invigorating waters of the New Testament; baptize him with a sense of the divine care and prove to him that Thou hast not ordained that he become a forgotten man."

In that tense, dramatic moment words of a poem trembled in consciousness. Looking upon a face that pain, disease had terribly ploughed and gashed for twenty years, I quoted the eight small lines.

"Gunnerson, I know a bit of verse you ought to know. It is titled 'By Night.' Listen a minute":

The tapers in the great God's hall
Burn ageless, beautiful and white,
But only with the fall of dusk
Disclose to earth their faithful light.

Earth keeps her lamps of beauty, too,
Fairer than stars in fields above;
Dark hours of grief and pain reveal
The undreamed constancy of love.

"Love has surrounded you, clasped you through all these hard, nigh unbearable years, Gunnerson. Many of your comrades have passed on. Where is F. D. R.? You are still here."

"I don't know for what reason," he acknowledged, again clutching at his left side.

"You will know. You will yet know the full meaning of the dark hours. Keep that little lamp of beauty burning. Don't let the last, flickering flame of beauty die. Who knows what can be—yet?"

Patting his shoulder, I turned to leave. He called wistfully through the now closed door: "Call again . . . soon."

Chauncey commenced to read the New Testament, underlining strong, powerful passages spoken by a Galilean peasant. He commenced writing little treatises and meditations on verses that enchanted him. The swelling in the right arm slowly subsided. Even the bad eye felt better.

Church friends called to visit him. Verne, lonely since his wife's death, found rare fellowship in Chauncey. Ladies carried food, deliciously cooked, well seasoned, into the upper room. Invitations came for him to be entertained in church homes. Sandy, the Scotsman, was crazy over him. Arlene and Al, newly in love, welcomed him into a brand-new room prepared especially for him.

One never-to-be-forgotten day a man who was again finding the will to believe, discovering that heaven was occupied, no longer empty, enjoying an old volume his mother read, drove an old black coupe up on the wide, shadowed church lawn.

Many, many astonished communicants in rural Connecticut watched him as he parked his car, moved toward the wide steps and, unaided, perhaps slowly, with labor—climbed the sun-haloed steps. He entered a restful Pilgrim sanctuary and slipped into a cushioned pew with an audible sigh.

What do you suppose we decided to sing from our Pilgrim hymnals that incredible Sunday? It was one of those rare, intuitive flashes a pastor has on special occasions: "Faith is the victory that overcomes the world."

A Day at the Polls

A minister can learn valuable lessons not communicated by universities and libraries while standing reverently twelve hours beside a busy voting machine, watching the townspeople as they come and go, making sure everything is done "decently and in order." This apostolic advice is certainly appropriate for rural voting booths!

It was a high privilege to act as custodian for one of Canterbury's two voting machines. I am looking now at my "election officer's certificate," issued by Norman Kerr, our first selectman. And my heart swells a bit as I remember the day and think of four eager and heroic foreign immigrants, now citizens, and realize what it cost them to pull the lever for the men of their choice.

My first experience was with a Finnish man over ninety

years of age, infirm and weak, his eyes failing. Relatives guided him into the new school where the town's people flocked. He came slowly down the aisle to the voting machine, a strong, resolute young man on each side, directing his progress. Silent, determined, with snowy head held high, he approached the booth and entered behind the curtains (not iron) of our Nutmeg state. One could see the pride and joy of his franchise scrawled across his ashen-grey, deeply fissured face.

With what a sense of privilege and high honor he stepped from behind the curtain and went on his way, having cast his vote for the destinies of his new country! Like an old soldier he marched forth into the bright November sunlight.

I was next impressed by an aged French lady, bowed beneath the weight of years, her iron-grey hair a witness to her age. She did not speak English easily. It was clear that she was a little bewildered by an intricate voting machine. Fortunately one of the men guarding our machines spoke fluent French. Instantly she began a solemn and crucial conversation with him.

"You will give me direction, please?"

Her words were a mixture of French and English. How should she use the levers? How could she get herself released from the curtain's privacy after she had finished her work? One could detect how excited and enthusiastic she was by the tone of voice and the sharp, explosive power of her words. She remained in the booth a considerable time. One knew that she was studying the great panorama behind the curtains with intensity and rising wonder. When she finally emerged, there was light and rapture upon her face and she walked down the corridor to the exit with the strength and poise of a conqueror!

The third person who impressed me was a comparatively

young man of Slavic origin, tall, unsteady, suffering from an incurable disease. I do not know how he happened to come to the school for the exercise of his new-found freedom. He was seldom seen outside his small cottage.

He was so unsteady on his legs that he came down the school hallway bracing himself against the wall. As he painfully inched forward I realized the heroism and courage of this determined young man.

The other three guarding the polls noticed the resolution of this lean, swaying one who, wincing with pain, fought his deliberate way to the first voting machine. His clothes were not of the Sunday-go-to-meeting texture. But there was a heroism in his approach that gave one a view of Valley Forge perhaps and of Gettysburg and the Argonne forest.

He grabbed hold of the voting machine as though it were a life raft on a perilous ocean. He pulled himself inside, closeted himself with his essential liberties, worked the levers and dragged himself outside and to the wall and toward the rear door. I watched him forcing his halting legs out into the schoolyard as though he had won the greatest battle of a long and strenuous career.

The fourth person was a Russian countess, a refugee from the Bolshevik revolution of many decades ago. She had met a captain of the wild Carpathian Cossacks as she fled across the Black Sea to Turkey. The lady with the grand manner wed the fierce, powerful ruler of the mountains. They have lived a quarter of a century on a rocky and scraggly back-road Canterbury farm.

The elegant lady is terribly crippled with arthritis, so again, I was surprised to find her at the polls, assisted by her towering, powerful husband, his scimitar-curved moustache grimly suggesting other things. He helped her to the booth and gave her advice about the proper use of the machine. She smiled with the sweetness and grace of a court lady as she recognized me, and hid herself behind a drawn curtain.

The bell rang—and we knew she had pulled the lever that locked her in. But in a few moments she spoke, vigorously, to her husband in Russian. She had used all her strength to pull the large lever. She did not have sufficient power to work the voting lever or to release herself from the booth. What to do?

Her lean, long-armed husband spoke to me. We did have a problem on our hands. The dear lady had literally imprisoned herself behind an American curtain, too weak and enervated to vote.

"Wait a moment," I told the Cossack. "We will take care of everything."

He thrust a Russian sentence in through the drawn curtains. I hurried to the official leaders of the balloting, men of both parties. They entered inside the shelter and followed her directives in operating the levers.

When she came forth she was panting, exhausted. Leaning heavily on the powerful arm of a Cossack she turned back to the corridor and the exit.

"That is good," she panted to her husband, whose lean, sinewy strength revealed a vision of the authority of his early years. She said something in Russian that we failed to understand; but the powerful man grinned from behind dark eyes and the scimitar-moustache danced at both ends. Their car was driven to the back door; she pulled herself inside and vanished.

I returned to the manse that night realizing what the privilege of voting means to those who have fought and bled and have become exiles to win it. My preacher-heart was thanking God late into the night for this vision of a vibrant, living America I had received during the initial year of activity as guardian and instructor at the great symbol of our high destinies—a voting machine.

Grove of Pines

A minister finds himself attached to a church for better, for worse, for richer, for poorer, in sickness and in health. I was suffering from a gloom of depression and felt that I should resign my pastorate when a chance visit to a remote farm challenged me to rethink my mission.

It was a bright, November day when I ventured into the hinterlands to call on a vegetable farmer. This particular day he did not talk about his excellent farm lands, the crops he had harvested and marketed, his production records.

"Ever see my grove of pines?" he asked. "Great big fellers! Been standing on the place a century or more. Think I'd sell 'em? Never!"

Finding that I was interested, this generally quiet, industrious farmer led me across the road and an eighth of a mile from the barn.

"The farmers around here think I'm crazy," he chuckled. "Won't sell my trees, not a one! I've been offered a small fortune for their lumber. Well, those trees won't be dismembered and sawed down to chicken coops. Not if I go to the poorhouse!"

"What good are they?" I inquired, a bit ignorantly.

"What good? Glory be! I just like to see the big fellers standing by the road. They'll be there long after I'm gone! They arrived long before me. What good? Glory be! I like to know they're there! No Yank farmer can grow one of them in a lifetime!"

I shall always remember the sun spilling through a beautiful green ceiling overhead, splashing upon the fragrant bark, running along the graceful boughs. Sunlight was evaporating a thin falling of snow from the night before. We tramped the cracking brush and dried leaves and moved about the throne-room of the giant pine kings.

"Look at 'em!" enthused my host, grinning, chuckling in his dry-as-dust manner. "Think you can put your arms around those fellers? Go on! Let's see you!"

I knew by glancing at the huge trunks that I would only waste my time and get an ironic grin if I tried.

"See those other smaller trees, all dying?" The farmer pointed to a clump of young oaks and maples.

"Why?" I inquired.

"Other trees can't live with the pines. They hog the sun for themselves and eat up all the grub the earth's got."

Gazing around at the gathering of forest kings, I thought of the poetic line: "I am monarch of all I survey."

"See how straight they are!" triumphed the farmer. "They stand even straighter than a parson!" He beckoned me to stand beside him at the base of one uprearing trunk. "Cast your eye along the length of that, right up! Talk about a pillar of the church! Run your eye right up to the sky! Straight as a plumb line to the very top!"

My friend was not generally so talkative as this. I was amazed. Even this afternoon he only talked by spasms. Vast chasms of silence split his paragraphs. His proud, challenging manner said more than his words. No one ever displayed his infants with more apparent pride and joy than this grey-haired Yankee codger as he tramped about his evergreen sanctuary.

They were his! They grew on his land! They belonged to his acres! Folks could stand and stare at them as they passed along the winding road. People would learn to thrill to them as he had!

"Fool farmers before my time on the place went and cut most o' the others down," he complained and groaned. "These few remains tell the story. Look!"

He pointed grimly into the debris that always litters a pine-grove floor. "Look!" He marked out a tree trunk twice the size of any tree standing. "Man! What pines used to be here and would still be if men let 'em alone. You know, parson, people like to tear things down they can't ever replace. Nation and church ain't the only places where fools bungle along and work agin their own best interests. A pretty general practice everywhere, I should say."

To confess, I was thrilled, excited by the gracefulness, the poetry, enthusiasm and devoutness of this aloof, gruff farmer as he moved slowly among his high-standing and unimpeachable friends and swore eternal loyalty to them, more by his proud, kingly manner than by his frequent bursts of adoration. There was a noble air about this man in his farm togs that I have recognized in few others—even among many distinguished men of the cloth. He had grown like the glorious, towering creatures with which he had been happily and affectionately associated.

My friend had been handicapped with back trouble in the summer. He now tramped the brush as spry as any man.

"You're walking better," I suggested.

"Yup, sure am. And glory be, why not? Been resting a mite lately. Just been learning, like these pines, not to bother my head over every contrary wind that blows." He searched my face. "You know, parson, lots o' church leaders would do better if they didn't get ruffled up over every contrary wind that blows. It's a great thing when a man grows up—grows up like one of these pines—and sticks his head up over all lesser things, underbrush and parasites and all and learns to enjoy the sunshine and let the clouds go by."

I am sure God sent me into that cloistered retreat to walk and talk with a seer. I left my friend that crisp November afternoon knowing I had received one of the greatest lectures ever delivered on life and dignity and good common sense. I had written my resignation to the church and had left it on my study desk. I hurried home and tossed it into the waste basket.

Yes, why not move up higher into the bright sunshine and let the contrary winds blow themselves out?

Prayer for the President

A headline in the *Hartford Times* of June 12, 1956, carried this message: "*Unaware, minister prayed for Ike, naming ailment.*"

I would like a word of introduction before we grapple with the story.

Any scientist must note, register and try to find a category for data, factual experience, however strange and cryptic the material. The scientific method is to observe phenomena, to find the fact, describe it and try to interpret it. Oftentimes years pass before the scientist can make a full explanation, if ever—for instance, interpretations of atomic motion, electricity, psychic manifestations.

I will simply relate the experience as it happened on a Friday evening in the Westminister Church. Some fifty people attended the prayer meeting.

Every week we asked the congregation to name special requests for prayer—people in trouble, ill, in hospitals, facing financial problems, delinquent children—and we asked the good Lord to help in every case. Six requests had been named and written down on an envelope when a tall, distinguished gentleman, sitting beside his gracious wife, pulled himself to his feet. He was Ralph Atkins of Gales Ferry, a man about sixty with greying hair. He worked for Electric Boat. He had recently enjoyed a ride on the atomic submarine, the *Nautilus*.

"I think we ought to have a prayer for the President," he announced. He said only this and sat down. My seventh request was written on the torn envelope: "President Eisenhower."

I enter into specific prayer as carefully as taking care of a business detail.

At noon a radio flash had mentioned the President's illness the night before, which suggested another possible heart attack. I had heard nothing about Mr. Eisenhower's condition from that hour.

At eight-thirty I commenced to pray for the seven special requests, the congregation uniting its faith with mine. Six prayers were "run of the mill," I shall say. But as I began to enter into the Eisenhower prayer, something happened. I suddenly realized a difference in interest, tempo, power. A perspiration started to cover me; a sort of heat seemed to engulf me and I still recall many things about the experience.

"O God and Father, have mercy on our Chief Executive. He cannot be spared at this time and he is very ill. If it's—but Lord, it isn't his heart. It's lower, lower, in his stomach. No, Lord, it's a blockage of the intestinal tract."

As I prayed it seemed the word "cancer" rose up before me, a black, hateful thing. An inner voice ordered: "Don't say it!" I cannot describe the eerie, soul-shattering experience of this particular moment.

"There's a blockage, Lord. Break it loose! Break it loose! Break it loose!" I was sharply conscious of a triune statement as the prayer became impassioned. The number three stood out in mind rather than the fact of repetition. Other things were said which have been forgotten. I remember finishing my prayer with these words, spoken to the congregation: "The President will be eased; he will feel better in the morning."

Church people, simple farmers, genial housewives, were astonished. My wife said she was "shaken" as I went into amazing detail concerning a sickness that no one divined. Why the pinpoint diagnosis? Was my zeal in prayer making me overemotional and romantic? I hardly knew what to think myself.

I did sense some kind of drama, some reality in it, followed soon by an elation of spirit. When retiring, two hours later, I found myself singing a well-known Negro spiritual in the dark of midnight:

> I know the Lord,
> I know the Lord,
> I know the Lord laid his hands on me.

I recall now, looking back, that it seemed I had somehow ministered to the deepest needs of our Chief Executive. An inner voice whispered: "Though but a poor rural pastor, far from the madding crowd's ignoble strife, you have had part in the vital story of the land you love; you have helped in a dark hour." As I had prayed it had seemed that, for a moment, I stood beside a bed in Walter Reed Hospital.

A good night's sleep interred the queer episode with yesterday's history. I glanced at a morning paper's black headline. The paper had gone to press at midnight.

Specialists had decided not to operate on the President. That was the headline. It occurred to me, on reading this, that I had been unduly excited over my prayer-ministry. Indeed, my wife was right; I was getting too enthusiastic in my parish efforts. I must simmer down.

An hour later, at eighty-thirty while I was eating a late breakfast, the radio news commentator made a special announcement: "Emergency operation for President Eisenhower following sudden night consultation. Non-cancerous obstruction of the intestinal tract. Operation successful. The President is resting comfortably."

My own words almost, spoken at eight-thirty the night before, had seemingly gone around the world and were coming back to me twelve hours later. For a moment I sat, stunned, at the breakfast table. My wife simply stared at me. I was staring at her.

"Did you hear—that?" I finally gasped.

"It . . . seems . . . impossible," she stammered.

Sunday morning fifty people attended church to tell fifty more about the bewildering moments of a rural prayer meeting.

Said Deacon Earl MacLeod of Windham, approaching me beside the front steps—the very spot where Arlene, Al and four children had stood—"I would write the President about the experience. It is really something to write about."

Monday I sat down and wrote my Chief Executive a letter. While typing it, I felt another strong impression upon me and a prophetic word hit me from the rapt Isaiah's seraphic fire. Isaiah 41:10 came to me with great power:

> Fear thou not; for I am with thee: be not dismayed; for I am thy God: I will strengthen thee; yea, I will help thee; yea, I will uphold thee with the right hand of my righteousness.

I remember writing him to continue, unhindered, on his way. I humbly believed he should remain in office and run again for the presidency. I felt he would win handsomely on another election and have no recurrence of his disease. I wrote him that a distant, unknown pastor and his flock thanked God that they seemed called in to hold up his hands on a critical night.

Monday I phoned a great Connecticut daily (not the *Times*): "Was the President undergoing the operation at three o'clock Saturday morning?" The triune phrase in the prayer seemed to indicate the number three.

The editor could scarcely conceal his disgust. What would a country parson know about an operation? He said his dispatches hadn't divulged the hour of surgery. He hung up on me. I only ask any interested reader of these pages to see how the number three figures for that tragic Saturday morning and to draw his own conclusions.

How did a handful of simple folk in a distant, ancient church, built six years before the American Revolution, seem to get an advance flash on world-crucial news and know—hours before the wisest surgical science made a decision—the true facts of the case?

Scientists think we preachers are crazy; I often say that even scientists have a long distance to travel yet.

Did I receive an answer to my letter to Mr. Eisenhower? Indeed I did, written on White House stationery, mailed from the Walter Reed Hospital. It carried a strong man's signature, a strong man even in convalescence. It is a prized possession of mine and it reads: Dwight D. Eisenhower.

How do I explain the experience?

I . . . don't . . . even . . . try.

[illegible] remember urging him to consider [illegible], on the [illegible]. I honestly believed he should [illegible] and the [illegible] for the presidency. I felt he would [illegible] another election and have no [illegible] to [illegible] than these [illegible], unimportant [illegible] [illegible] then these seemed [illegible] to hold up his [illegible] on a [illegible] [illegible].

[illegible] I planned a great [illegible] [illegible]. [illegible] "Will the President undergoing [illegible] [illegible] [illegible] [illegible] Saturday morning?" The [illegible] phrase in the [illegible] seemed to indicate the number three.

The editor could scarcely conceal his [illegible]. What would a country parson know about an operation? He said [illegible] [illegible] had not divulged the hour of surgery. He [illegible] [illegible] I only asked my interested readers [illegible] [illegible] to see how the [illegible] these figures for that tragic Saturday morning and to draw their own conclusions.

How did a [illegible] or simple folk [illegible] [illegible] church, hold [illegible] before the [illegible] [illegible], [illegible] [illegible] [illegible] on [illegible] [illegible] [illegible] [illegible] the [illegible] surgical [illegible] [illegible] [illegible]— [illegible] of the [illegible]?

[illegible] think we [illegible] are [illegible] [illegible] [illegible] [illegible] a long distance [illegible]

[illegible] an answer to my letter to [illegible] were [illegible] at White House [illegible] [illegible] [illegible] Walter Reed Hospital [illegible] [illegible] [illegible] [illegible] [illegible] Dwight D. Eisenhower.

[illegible] the experience?

[illegible]

Chimes and Christmas Capers

I must say a word about our happiest, holiest season before I end this recital.

For many, many years it seemed I moved empty-handed toward the sermon barrel at the thrilling hour of the Nativity; the idea of "The Child" failed to lay proper hands upon me. I knew there were things to say that I didn't say; there was something to feel I just didn't feel!

A kind lady, a department store clerk of the greying years, rescued my Yule-log sermons and to this day never suspects a thing!

God love her, the stout, solemn-faced, tired-eyed clerk of a widespread department store of three floors, with eyes to see, ears to hear, alert with woman's unerring intuition.

I was entertaining two little tots who were literally tearing a nursery apart while a weary young mother shopped in the furniture section. We were laughing, frolicking, having the time of our lives.

The stout lady who sold window curtains and drapes spoke to the assistant manager who passed along the busy floor. She pointed toward a boisterous nursery.

"Look at that!" she enthused. "Look at his height! Look at his build! Hear that laugh! See him with those little rascals! You don't have to advertise for a Santa Claus. You have one and he's a natural!"

"Hm-m," grunted the manager. "Yes, that could be our man."

A genial, polished gentleman approached.

"Ever play Santa Claus?"

Yes, that was the origin to an experience in a lively city store not many miles from rural Canterbury; it was my real introduction to the bright and beautiful traffic of Christmas. And in eight years I was ministering to no less than five thousand children!

The carpenters built me a huge throne-chair on the third floor, surrounded by a glittering toyland; the window-dresser tacked intriguing stars to the painted walls, planted artificial trees; the boss stuffed my impressive scarlet bag with gifts and candies. My inseparable pal, Rudolph, stood, guarding the way to my feet.

For one month in twelve I really came into my own—monarch of all I surveyed—a rural parson of the far-flung wilderness. See to what a dizzy eminence Life has whirled the country pastor! In blazing red suit and cap, in glistening black belt and boots, in white moustache and beard, carrying my exciting pack bulging with all sort of intriguing things, I held high office for Christmas, Children and Company. It was a wonderful, memorable experience to be a part of childhood's world of faith, hope and love. Often I wished for the power to grant every desire that came from the heart.

Some youngsters came back again and again breathlessly to add to the list of things they wanted. But some thought about other people, too. One boy moved shyly to my throne to ask:

"Santa, where do you sleep?"

"Up in the air, or on some rooftop, or at the North Pole."

"Isn't it cold up there, Santa?"

"Not so bad."

"Santa, I'm going home. I've got a big bed and it's warm. I'm going to ask my father if I can't have you sleep with me." And he scampered away before I could stop him.

A little girl accepted a candy cane from my pack, then pried some hard candies from her pocket and offered them to me.

"You give things to children, Santa," she said, "but who gives things to you?"

A bigger boy said he didn't believe in Santa Claus.

"You are a fake, Santa!" he blurted to the toy department. I let him tug at my eyebrows—my own but whitened. They didn't come off and he seemed surprised. He showed up again next day, still suspicious. In the crowd I spied an aged and wrinkled lady.

"Hello, Ada!" I called to her. She recognized my voice and almost divulged my identity. My raised finger stopped her in the nick of time. "You've known me for a hundred and fifty years, haven't you?" I asked and nodded toward the open-mouthed boy.

"No, for two hundred!" she flourished.

The youngster stared at her white hair and deeply creased cheeks, then he turned to me.

"Gee, Santa, you *are* real, ain't you? I'm sorry I acted the way I did. Only, Santa, every year I told you to bring me a two-wheeler bicycle and you never did. Will I get one this time?" I looked on him—a child of the tenements.

One little girl said she wanted a baby sister or brother for Christmas. With only a glance at her mother, I could solemnly promise delivery, though I did explain it might not be exactly on December 25. The flustered, smiling mother hurried her daughter away.

"There ain't no Santa Claus!" taunted a group of teen-aged girls. It was a chance I very seldom missed.

"God is the real Santa Claus," I countered. "He gives us the good and never-failing gifts of sun and wind and rain, our food, our homes, our parents, our friends and little children." The girls became quiet and reverent and a little tot, reassured, moved over to stroke the fur on my coat.

"What makes you so big, Santa?" one puny youngster of four years asked one afternoon. His mother whispered in my ear.

"Eating my breakfasts," I informed him. "Oh, I go for milk in a big way, Jackie! And I'll bet you don't eat your oatmeal. And how about your vegetables?" The following year Jackie came to see me again—and he was eating—and what a change Santa's dietary talk had made!

One dusk I was on the loading platform in the rear of the store. I heard loud crying. Up the street I spied a boy slashing at a girl's legs with a whip. I rushed up to them. Neither observed my approach.

"Heh, you!" I said gruffly.

The lad about twelve turned around and his eyes all but popped from their sockets. The whip fell from his hand.

"Wha . . . wha . . . what . . . you . . . doin' . . . here?" he chattered.

"I'm everywhere. Now what are you, a big boy, doing, hitting a girl?" I grabbed a shoulder.

"She . . . she's . . . m-m-m-y sis . . . ter and . . . she . . . won't . . . g-g-go . . . home."

"All the worse, to hit a sister."

I drew a juicy, cellophane-wrapped candy cane from my impressive pack and handed it to the speechless little girl, who snatched it and ran down the street.

"You don't deserve one," I informed the lad, "and I ought not to bring you one single toy for Christmas."

"G . . . gosh," groaned the youngster, "I on . . . only. . . ."

"But here," I relented. "You forgot yourself. I'll forgive you this time. You really didn't mean to hurt your sister, did you?"

"N . . . n . . . no," he gasped, shot forth a hand, grabbed the cane I offered and raced after the vanishing girl. I am sure he improved in the fine art of brotherhood from that hour.

One day a dignified, well-dressed lady in her forties joined the line of children and moved slowly to my throne.

"Santa," she suggested, "am I too big to make a wish?"

"One is never too big, too old to make a wish."

"Santa, will you please send back my son, my only child, for Christmas? I am a widow—he's in . . . Korea." She stuffed her handkerchief in her mouth and made a hasty exit from the madcap toyland.

Another day a girl of nine or ten brought drama to the steady feet of Rudolph. A man and a woman pushed a thin, very handsome girl toward me.

"Cecelia, it's your turn now," said the lady, apparently the mother. "Tell Santa what you want for Christmas."

She stretched a long, graceful arm and shooks hands. Her smile was a beautiful thing to see. Dark, lustrous eyes searched mine; I could feel the lovely impact.

"Santa, do you know what I'd really like to have you do for me this Christmas?"

"Yes, Cecelia, of course."

"Would you please send my real daddy back to me? He's in California, and I love him so. Will . . . you . . . go . . . and . . ."

She burst into tears and the lady, glaring at the child and at me, looking dumbstruck at the man beside her, grabbed that girl by the hand and pulled and tugged her away.

A few days later a gracious, wistful little girl of four edged toward my chair. Her thick brunette hair was like a halo about her dark skin. She was Jewish. I held out a hand. The darling thing rushed into my arms with a glad cry, "Oh, Santa!" She twined beautiful fingers about my neck, kissed my beard.

The mother was frightened. For an instant a look of panic suffused her. She reached for the thoughtless child. I had risen from my throne and was now hugging the child and starting a little stroll with her among my starry expanse.

"Don't be alarmed," I advised the mother. "She's a glorious child and she comes from the magic land of the first Christmas."

Never can a man describe the easing of tension, the smile of peace that haloed a woman's face beneath the tinsel stars of a twentieth-century department store.

It was real fun one day when the Polish photographer took a shot of me with a colored child of three on one knee, an Eskimo girl of five on the other, a Chinese boy in the middle. It was thrilling to hold tiny infants, three months old, six months, to be photographed and their pictures—and mine—to go to soldier-fathers in army camps across the seven seas!

One of my most exciting moments was on a busy Saturday

morning. A plump, sweet-faced girl, Yvonne, a vision of orchid and green in the most enchanting snowsuit I have ever seen, stood in my presence. She gave me her list for Christmas. Mother and grandmother stood behind her and both said: "Now tell Santa what your father told you he wanted for Christmas."

Talk about the eloquence of silence! Here it was. She did not divulge a word. A half-dozen times they prodded her as she shook her head and grunted disapproval.

"Go on, Yvonne; go on, Yvonne, tell Santa."

Finally the darling child, out of patience, exclaimed: "I won't! I won't! Daddy'll only get drunk and spoil all my fun for Christmas."

I lifted up the resolute child and gave her a big kiss and said to the grinning ladies, "You know, folks, this Santa Claus happens to be a minister of the gospel."

"A what?" gasped the mother.

"Not a preacher!" howled the elderly lady. "Oh, dear!"

How fast that little group of three melted into thin air!

I served as Santa three years at the large Polish parochial school. A store clerk, an official there, prevailed on the Polish-American Club to pay my expenses for the entire morning as I covered eight grades in the school. I sat at parochial pianos to play and sing the carols with the various grades. In the nursery tiny, darling displaced children from Warsaw thronged me, danced about me and let me hug and kiss them and waltz them around the sacred floors.

One of my richest experiences as Santa came when the store's assistant manager, Harry Sturtevant, suggested that I distribute the gifts at a home for some poor children in the vicinity. I'll not forget the eager, anxious little faces that became smiling as I handed each child a package.

"Thank you so much, Santa Claus! You didn't forget us, did you? You are a good Santa Claus!"

Of course after four weeks of excitement, letters, voices, requests, prayers, the children wore me to a frazzle. January meant a floored, exhausted Saint Nick back on the winter hills in a parish house. Once or twice I was all winter recovering from the attack of Christmas.

However, let me admit this.

After I had placed twenty-five hundred handsome, wistful boys on my knees; after I had hugged and blessed twenty-five hundred little girls, I moved forward in confidence and strength toward the church's Christmas candles and bell. No longer did Christmas Eve plague me with a full moon and empty arms. Somehow I felt ready, equipped to minister before the mystic and wonderful crypt of God's Child.

Epilogue

PRAYER OF A PASTOR

Keep my heart always young enough to love,
To share a child's bright sense of wonder when
The great moon swings between the dark and dawn
And ocean-trumpets wake the flowered glen.
Let my soul know when beauty rustles by
And treasure, ever, what her hands have sown;
Should I grow old, keep me in spirit free,
Nor grudge the bridal though I walk alone.
Let not the strife for gain dull eyes to miss
The ageless wealth heaped by a cedar-rill;
Though ears grow used to barter they must not
Lose vaster echoes on a wind-strewn hill.
Let some kind accident convey me hence
The night before my dream-world falls away—
If ever it must fall. How could I live
A creditable life beyond that day?
I would expect new loveliness each hour—
A child in heart so long as I have breath,
Swayed by new faces and all happy things!
And grant to me some ecstasy in death.

THREE CHURCHES AND A MODEL T

PHILIP JEROME CLEVELAND

This is a book filled with the heart-warming adventures of a country preacher as he travels the highways and byways, bringing God and His church to the people.

In relating experiences culled from a lifetime of loyal service to the country church, Philip Jerome Cleveland shares with his reader *true* stories about *real* people. Here is the story of a truck driver inspired to action by a church which had stopped "talking"; of the trials a preacher faced with his borrowed Model T when his own car vanished in a dense New England fog;

continued on back flap